Managing
Upside
Down

Also by Tom Chappell

The Soul of a Business

Managing
Upside
Down

The Seven Intentions of
Values-Centered Leadership

TOM CHAPPELL

William Morrow and Company, Inc.
New York

Library of Congress Cataloging-in-Publication Data has been applied for

ISBN 0-688-17069-2

Printed in the United States of America

First Edition

1 2 3 4 5 6 7 8 9 10

BOOK DESIGN BY BERNARD KLEIN

www.williammorrow.com

This book is dedicated with my thanks to six men whose time, love, and example have given me dimension.

To my father, George, who taught me courage;

To my Bishop, Fred Wolf, who shared his wisdom;

To my counselor, Fred Scribner, who taught me prudence;

To my coach in commerce, John Rockwell, who encouraged me to dream;

To my teacher, Dick Niebuhr, who guided me towards discovery and reflection;

To my friend, Dick Spencer, who believed in me.

Contents

Acknowledgments

I am grateful for the many people who have contributed to the creation of this book. Our collaborations are a testament to the power of teamwork in producing something good and effective.

I especially want to thank Ed Tivnan who helped me write this book. From my chapter outlines and numerous tapes of spoken manuscript, Ed has crafted a concise, fast-moving, and dramatic text. He has been a joy to work with.

I also want to thank Jerry Pieh who helped me assemble my first thoughts and early draft. His confidence in my ideas was essential to the early stage of the book.

The book is enhanced by the many people who have contributed individual pieces. My wife, Kate, Tom O'Brien, John Rockwell, Dan Erickson, Melissa Skelton, Cindy Angerhofer, and Jim Newcomb have provided important voices to the value of the Seven Intentions, to Tom's of Maine, and to the Saltwater Institute. I thank each of them.

I want to thank my business colleagues in Boulder who provided the opportunity for the Seven Intentions to evolve. Their willingness and confidence in me made my crafting of the Seven Intentions all the more efficacious.

To Jim Levine, my agent, I give thanks for the chance to create another product together. His confidence in me and his insights for the vision of the book have been valuable.

And to my editor, Zach Schisgal, I thank you for your confidence in the book.

Introduction

This is a book for people who want to do business with their hearts as well as their heads. For most wise men of commerce, such a statement is a contradiction in terms: Business is not social work, they'll tell you; it's about making more money this quarter than last. Period. Profit is king! I'm sure you know all the arguments as well as I do. But what I also know, firsthand and beyond a doubt, is that I have been running our company, Tom's of Maine, according to a mission of respecting customers, employees, community, and the environment, and we are creating more products and making more money than I ever dreamed.

I call it "Managing Upside Down"—letting your own deepest beliefs and values, not just the bottom line, drive your business. I used to think that I could hire smart, ambitious professional managers, hand them a copy of our mission statement, and put them to work. But over the past few years, as I and this company have struggled to integrate our values into our business practices, I came to realize that people have to be trained in this values-centered approach; indeed, they have to be transformed into a new breed of manager, one by one. For unless you are absolutely committed to managing by values, unless it has become part of who you are, at the first sign of crisis, you will begin worrying more about the bottom line than the mission. I saw it happen at Tom's of Maine; I myself have been sucked back into the numbers game.

So I have devised the Seven Intentions of Values-Centered Leadership, a seven-step program to help my managers—and you—master managing upside down. In my business travels, at speaking engagements, or just running into old friends and college classmates, I hear the same story: No matter how fast the track they're on, even if they're already sitting on top of the pyramid as CEO or owner, the men and women I meet are still unhappy. In their heads, they may believe business is only about making money, but their hearts are telling them there ought to be more. Successful beyond their dreams and, in some cases, richer than Croesus, they can't get rid of the feeling that something is missing.

I know the feeling. In 1986, as the company my wife, Kate, and I founded, Tom's of Maine, was experiencing unprecedented growth, I was miserable. The young professionals whom I had hired to grow the company were taking it in directions I was not sure I wanted to go. In spite of the big house, the sailboat, five great kids, and a loving wife who was also my business partner, I realized that moving fast and fat did not fulfill me. I seriously considered cashing in and leaving the business world altogether. Instead, I retreated to the Harvard Divinity School, where for the next four years I juggled my work for a master's degree in theology with my duties as a husband, father, and confused manager of what was then a $5 million company. Surprisingly, reading the great theologians and philosophers actually rekindled my passion for business and creating good products; my stint in divinity school clarified my own intuition that I did not have to set aside my religious beliefs and my respect for people and the environment—in short, my *values*—to succeed in business. I set out, with the help and encouragement of my board and family, to place these values at the center of our company.

I wrote about that experience in *The Soul of a Business* (Bantam,

1993). Today, I am more committed than ever to what I have come to call a "values-centered" approach to corporate management. The company that Kate and I founded on $5,000 and a prayer is now the nation's leader in natural personal care products, with $30 million in sales as of 1999 and counting. We are now launching an entirely new business—Tom's of Maine's Natural Wellness Center—that will add to our brand a variety of natural medicines and herbal supplements to fight colds, prevent illness, and promote our customers' wellness from the time they wake up in the morning until they go to bed at night, more than seventy new products.

This was never, of course, my goal. In fact, I never had any ultimate goal in mind. How could I? While trying to build Tom's of Maine, I was also struggling with my own personal and professional identity. But in the process of searching for my own soul, I found the soul of my business. We succeeded differently, by attracting customers who shared our beliefs and values and then passed the word on to their friends and neighbors. We made an emotional connection to our customers and developed it, motivating us to build this business toward greater service and value. All kinds of awards came our way, statewide, regional, and national. Incredible amounts of ink were expended on Tom's of Maine—newspaper articles, magazine covers, and a story in *The New York Times Magazine*. People were asking me who my public relations company was. The fact was, we didn't have one; we still don't. Our advertising budget is one tenth that of our competitors. Yet the word about Tom's of Maine got around. What is truly remarkable about all this attention is that Tom's of Maine became famous for simply doing the right thing. Integrating our values into our business strategies appealed to everyone—customers, the press, the community, and all sorts of people who wanted to work for a values-oriented company. Along the way, Tom's of Maine has become a kind of laboratory for what I believe will be a new paradigm for corporate America that will replace inflexible autocracies with a partnership between managers and their employees, building value by values. I really believe that, and I am not alone. Ralph Larsen, the chairman of Johnson & Johnson, generously told *The New York Times* that Tom's of Maine was "charting a new course."

It is usually at this point that my audience turns skeptical: Surely you don't expect me to go to divinity school? Of course not. You have a business to run, numbers to make, shareholders to excite, a board of directors to please. Another common concern I hear: All this talk about values is nice, at least in theory, but too often getting to the top of the pyramid requires being a natural-born killer. Can I, at this stage of the game, suddenly stop throwing my weight around? Can an old dog like me learn to share power?

Yes—and to that end, consider this book a kind of "tool kit." *Managing Upside Down* will explain how any manager, religious or not, can reorient his focus from a single-minded obsession with the bottom line to integrating values with the pursuit of profit. Once values begin driving your business, destiny will knock on your door, opening up opportunities that were unimaginable to you just a few years ago. In this book, I will help you establish what your values are and tell you how you can build them into the center of every business plan. I will give you a way to escape your tendencies to be a know-it-all and tap into your company's biggest, and least expensive, creative resource: your employees. We're all conscious about limiting risks. But I've discovered that you can build a company without limits by encouraging employees to explore new ideas and business opportunities. No matter whether we operate from the big corner office or from a spot on the assembly line, everyone in the business world is held accountable. Too often, however, accountability is a negative, fearful process, fostering an us-against-them attitude. I will show you how to set up small management teams where each idea is assessed according not to one person's idea of success, but to how it gets the whole team to its goal.

Let me assure you, we have a lot in common. Yes, Tom's of Maine is a successful company. But our success did not happen overnight, and we have faced considerable obstacles all along the way. Kate and I started out in 1970 mixing vats of detergent with a two-by-four; our first "breakthrough" nonpolluting natural detergent had one problem—it didn't work. Just seven years ago, when our company was enjoying unprecedented growth and acclaim, I reformulated a new deodorant for ecological reasons and was horrified to discover that the change caused half the users to smell worse rather than better; if that weren't bad enough, we recalled the deodorant, a decision (my decision) that cost the company $400,000—30 percent of our projected profits for that fiscal year.

So I am no stranger to failure and humiliation. Sure, I am a religious man who is also passionate about conserving the environment. But I am also a CEO, with all the bad habits and attitudes that are natural to the species. Even after almost a decade of lecturing and writing about my belief that corporate America has to junk its autocratic, know-it-all tendencies and partner up with our so-called subordinates, I am still as naturally self-interested, overconfident, full of pride, and eager to control a meeting as any CEO in America. Every day, I struggle with my ego. If an aging Yankee entrepreneur like me, raised on the virtues of individualism and self-reliance, can learn a little humility and to depend on others, so can you.

And if you doubt the benefits of sharing power, *Managing Upside Down* will give you examples of how when you encourage your employees to speak up, they can contribute to the bottom line, big-time. Like the time we had a glitch in manufacturing our deodorant and our engineers came up with a solution that would cost $20,000. One of the guys on the assembly line had another idea—which cost $49. It worked perfectly, and we still use it. If my head of manufacturing was a tyrant, do you think that guy would have piped up? Similarly, I will show you how by decreasing our R&D group to several three-person teams a year ago, we have increased our product development *tenfold* and are forging ahead into an entirely new business.

Values-centered leadership is hardly a science; it is a trial-and-error process, and we have made our share of mistakes. This book will help you benefit from them. One of the biggest mistakes I made was to think that because I was so focused on Tom's of Maine's mission, all my top executives were, too. I will tell you the story of how getting everyone back on track (which required pushing a few of my top people off the track) took such a toll that a couple of years ago my family and I agreed to begin exploring selling Tom's of Maine—and why we didn't. It all revolved around sticking to our values. Values, too, played an extraordinary (I'm inclined to say "miraculous") role in attracting a young Procter & Gamble star to become our COO. I'll tell you the story of how I found him, and I'll let him tell the story of why he walked away from running an $850 million division of Procter & Gamble to join me in my adventure to let values drive our business and help others do the same.

Notice that I did not say let *only* values drive your business. I am talking about commerce, not church; and in business, if you don't make a profit, you will be soon out of business, no matter how good a person or socially responsible you might be. *Managing Upside Down* requires a dual focus, on values as well as profit. And the most important value of all is providing our customers with effective and appealing products.

"Values." Lately, people have been throwing that word around a lot. Politicians talk about "traditional values" and "family values"; business school professors lecture about "corporate values" and "business ethics"; CEOs have put their beliefs and values down on paper in the form of corporate "credos," "statements of beliefs," and "mission statements." But what exactly are "values"?

Values are what we as individuals, family members, and productive citizens consider important in life, what we want to pass on to our children and our communities. People's basic values, of course, differ. Some, for example, value making money over everything; profit, therefore, is their overriding value. If you think there's more to life than making money, if something is missing in your successful career, if you, like us at Tom's of Maine, believe in respecting your customers, employees, and community, then the Seven Intentions are for you.

A warning label: Transforming your corporate culture to values-centered leadership is demanding, time-consuming, and frustrating. At first, you might spin your wheels; you might even fail. We did both at Tom's of Maine. Be prepared for enormous obstacles and determined opposition. Your colleagues, board members, executives, managers, assistants, and the kid who wheels in the coffee cart will argue persuasively against this; they will show you stacks of spreadsheets and financial projections that will give you pause. They will wear you down. It happened to me. Some days, you will wonder whether you really belong in the business world; other days you'll think you're just plain crazy. I've been there, and my advice is: Stick with the Seven Intentions, for if you try to manage with your heart as well as your head, you will be amazed by the results. And so will the naysayers around you, at least the honest ones who in time will become converts to values-centered leadership for the most persuasive argument there is in business: It works.

The Seven Intentions program opens people to more potential, more energy, and fuller dimensions. These simple steps help channel purpose more effectively; they will increase productivity and accomplishment. Above all, the Seven Intentions will help you build a community in your workplace. One final warning: The Seven Intentions will also change your life. They turn talkers into listeners, egomaniacs into collaborators. I know, because it happened to me. I am a different person, and you will be, too.

But before you can take the first step to mastering *Managing Upside Down,* you have to reorient yourself away from thinking that successful managing is making more dough this quarter than last; you will have to redefine leadership for your company, abandoning the corporate hierarchy where the boss is always right for a partnership between you and your employees; above all, you will have to establish your set of values and commit yourself to them without compromise. These are some of the subjects of *Managing Upside Down.*

So let's begin.

1

Reorientation

In 1996, *The New York Times Magazine* published a fair and detailed account about my efforts at Tom's of Maine to create a new way of doing business. The article wondered whether our brand of what *The Times* writer called "socially responsible capitalism" made sense for other companies, and then let people like ex-Secretary of Labor Robert Reich and Arnold Hiatt, the former CEO of Stride Rite, argue that it did. But Al Dunlap, the notorious cost-cutter who was then chairman of Sunbeam, also interviewed by *The Times,* disagreed. "Business is not a social experiment," said Dunlap, who as CEO of Scott Paper downsized more than eleven thousand employees to make the company more attractive for takeover (earning the nickname "Chainsaw Al"). "You're in business to make money for your shareholders."

I disagree—so much, in fact, that over the past decade I have transformed my own company, Tom's of Maine, into a successful, well-known counterexample to the 350-year-old premise of capitalism that the self-interested pursuit of profit is king. I want to prove that we ought to be putting our social and environmental responsibilities before our pursuit of profit. Don't get me wrong. The marketplace is not church. Business is definitely about making money. But it is not *only* about making money. And while commerce may not be a social experiment, it is certainly filled with social responsibilities.

I suspect that you are reading this book because you, too, feel that there must be more to life (and work) than being a slave to the bottom line. It is an urge that goes against everything that you have been taught. Everyone has told you that if you want to do good, farm yourself out to the nonprofit world. I know the frustration—and I came close to quitting business altogether because of it.

Back in the mid-1980s I was a successful entrepreneur in the midst of a full-scale mid-life crisis. I was so fed up with the numbers game that I began seriously thinking of becoming a minister. Ironically, once I was in divinity school, I could not stop being a businessman. The lectures I heard and the great books I read were filtered through my point of view as CEO of Tom's of Maine. Happily, my theology studies seemed to confirm my own intuitions about how business ought to be done—from the heart as well as by the brain, according to your values as well as with an eye on the bottom line.

My big breakthrough came in a class in American religious philosophy taught by Richard R. Niebuhr, Hollis Professor of Divinity at Harvard, discussing an idea from the legendary fire-breathing Puritan preacher Jonathan Edwards: "Being is relation"—that is, by the very nature of our existence we are not separate, isolated entities, but always individuals with some kind of relationship with others. Immediately, it occurred to me that corporations, too, contrary to their legal status as distinct entities, could not avoid relationships with other entities—their customers, employees, suppliers, community, government, environment, and the future.

And social relationships bring responsibilities, moral as well as financial: What do the owners expect of a company in return for their financial investment? What do lenders expect of us? Employees? Customers? The community? Every responsible CEO wants to generate the highest possible return for the shareholders, but not by taking advantage of his workers or cheating his suppliers. No business wants to pollute the air or nearby streams. Every company prefers its own community to be safe, with good schools and social services. Thanks to Jonathan Edwards, I realized that far from being an amoral activity aimed at maximizing shareholder interests, business was by its very nature a social enterprise and therefore a moral enterprise.

In 1989, I convened my board of directors for a weekend of discussions about what a company like ours ought to be. The two sides of the issue were quickly evident: "Hey, this is business; it's about profit," argued some board members, while others said: "No business has the right to run roughshod over people or deplete the environment at the current rate of consumption. There are limits." Where my allegiance lay was not in doubt. That weekend my board and I came to the understanding that we could be true to both intuitions about how to run a company—for profit and for the common good. It was the origin of our corporate mission to be socially and environmentally responsible while being financially successful, and thus a profound moment in the history of Tom's of Maine. (See the Appendix.)

After that weekend, we began to fashion a new kind of company, and I think we have made remarkable progress. A decade ago, we were known for our natural toothpaste. Today, we're known for our great natural products *and* for our corporate values. We began by encouraging our employees to spend 5 percent of their paid company time volunteering in the community and by committing 10 percent of our pretax profits to nonprofit organizations. In the early years of our philanthropy, when our profits were modest, we made small grants to environmental and community groups in Maine and Massachusetts. As the company has grown, so has the scale and breadth of its donations. Giving money to worthy causes has become a big and serious job at Tom's of Maine. We now divide our grants into four areas: Education, Arts, Human Need, and the Environment. We give out forty to fifty grants a year, ranging from a multiyear

$100,000 pledge to the Harvard Divinity School's new Center for the Study of Values in Public Affairs and a $25,000 pledge to the Maine Audubon Society's Environmental Education Outreach Programs to $1,000 to help an elementary school in Maine design an outdoor classroom to teach kids about the natural world.

Recently, we have given grants to local arts organizations who encourage the work of disabled people and seniors. I'm particularly proud of our support of the Portland, Oregon–based River Network's efforts to assist groups around the country in organizing efforts to protect regional watersheds. In 1997, we began a multiyear grant of $100,000 to the New York–based Rainforest Alliance for its efforts to assist grass-roots programs around the world to conserve and sustain tropical forests. Last year, we gave $6,000 to the American Indian Institute for this Montana-based group's annual summit of elder Native Americans and their young people from all over the country to discuss issues affecting the nation's indigenous people. This year Maine's Native Americans will host this "Traditional Circle of Indian Elders and Youth," and we're proud to help out.

Every year, we work hard to select the most deserving organizations for our grants. Sometimes, however, the need is obvious. In April 1999, in the first weeks of the crisis in Yugoslavia over the fate of Kosovo, Tom's of Maine sent fifty thousand bars of soap to the Red Cross for the Kosovar families forced from their homes and communities.

When we devised a company policy to help people and groups in our community and other parts of the country a decade ago, we did so because it seemed the right thing to do. Amazingly, within a few years, we realized that such acts of social responsibility were so appealing to a growing group of consumers that what we thought was the right thing to do also became a profitable thing to do, too. Customers want a good product, but given the choice, they will buy the good product made by a company whose social and environmental concerns are the same as theirs. There are millions of such values-conscious customers, and by discovering them, we also had discovered that we could build the equity of our company by following our company's mission. In short, we began to build value by values, and I was amazed.

I had stumbled into Managing Upside Down.

WHAT EXACTLY IS "MANAGING UPSIDE DOWN"?

It's putting your social and moral responsibilities at the center of your business enterprise. It's putting your own ego aside and listening to your employees, collaborating with them, encouraging their creativity, all the while being guided by your values. Above all, Managing Upside Down is never making a move without consulting your values, and then sticking to them heart and soul.

But how can you follow your heart without getting your brains battered in the marketplace? It is not easy. Managing by values is a revolutionary way of doing business, and it won't happen by half-measures. If you are serious about learning to manage by values, you will have to throw a lot of what passes for conventional wisdom in the business world over the side. You will have to create new habits. In fact, you will have to change your whole mindset toward the marketplace. Above all (and here's the really hard part), you must learn to do two apparently contradictory things at once: follow your values and still make money. Instead of being focused only on profit, market share incentives, dividends, and building wealth, you must start thinking about doing some good for others. More difficult still, leading by values requires successful managers to set aside their pride as masters of their domain and turn themselves into servants of their ideals and values.

Managing Upside Down is not just a job; it's a vocation.

MANAGING BY VALUES IS REALLY AS AMERICAN AS APPLE PIE

Thinking about business from the point of view of your values seems almost un-American. ''The chief business of the American people is business,'' Calvin Coolidge famously said. But the business of American business has not always been so narrowly focused on making money. In early America, corporations were chartered by states as legal entities whose foremost duty was to the public interest. Many of the great families whose businesses helped build America in the nineteenth century and aimed the country toward undreamed-of prosperity in the twentieth century were aware of their social responsibilities.

I like to think that this American tradition of compassionate capitalism is in the bloodline of Tom's of Maine. My wife Kate's family, the Cheneys, created a silk company in an area outside of Hartford, Connecticut, in the 1830s. When their original idea of growing silkworms on mulberry trees was frustrated by the Northeast's climate, Kate's ancestors began importing silk from China and weaving it in their own mill. By the turn of the century, "Cheneyville" had become headquarters to the largest silk cloth producer in the Western world, the Cheney Silk Company. The family prospered, but not at the expense of their employees. Like many successful, God-fearing American merchants of those days, they believed a business had to give something back to the community, which was also their community. They built decent housing for their employees not far from their own homes. (Kate grew up in company housing, a compound of homes that were heated by steam from the mill boilers.) The women of the family, who were quite well educated for those days, created schools and financed the town library. Cheney cousins read to the women mill workers. The family also built a music hall, which is still in use, and invested funds to maintain the town cemetery. That money continues to be used for philanthropic work today. The family's reputation as a progressive employer attracted workers from all over New England.

Cheneyville did not happen by chance. Kate's family set out to create a mill town that was a kind of manufacturing utopia based on their own sense of a social mission. The old Cheney mills still stand as registered National Historical Sites as part of the town of Manchester, Connecticut. It is a remarkable part of American social and economic history. The Cheneys, of course, were not alone. Less than a century ago, other successful American families played an equally strong role in the towns that sprang up as part of the American Industrial Revolution. Curiously, though, it is the lives of the more predatory American businessmen that we seem to remember today, "The Robber Barons" who exploited workers, invented ingenious stock-manipulating schemes, and began the trend toward Big Business for the sake of nothing but bigness.

As another American century comes to a close, Tom's of Maine is searching for ways to *serve* our own employees, customers, and community for the twenty-first century. As proof of our commitment, the whole company recently turned away, I am amazed to say, from a process that would have yielded tens of millions of dollars and financial independence based on a gut feeling that our journey had many more interesting destinations to come. We had to carry on.

OUR BIGGEST BUSINESS DECISION EVER

By mid-1993, Tom's of Maine was not growing as well as we had thought. The year before, I had risked fiddling with the ingredients for our natural deodorant, with the catastrophic result that the deodorant gave odor-causing bacteria a better home *50 percent* of the time. After a healthy dialogue about our options, my managers and I decided that a company with a written mission that vows "to serve our customers by providing safe, effective, innovative, natural products of high quality" could not live with a defective deodorant on the shelves. Part of our mission is also "to build a relationship with our customers that extends beyond product usage to include full and honest dialogue." The right thing to do was to recall the deodorant from the stores, sending letters of apology to customers along with either a refund or the new product. The recall cost us $400,000—30 percent of our projected profits for that year.

Eighteen months later, the deodorant fiasco was still plaguing us. We had definitely lost our momentum at a time when the same companies that had once tried to buy us were now marketing a baking soda toothpaste and other "natural" products, with promotional budgets that dwarfed our own. Worse, I was discovering that my senior management viewed all this not through our mission, but through our budget. Their attitude was, "Sales were not going as planned, and the budget had to be cut to protect the bottom line." When the crunch came, my managers were scrambling for the lifeboats, and the first thing to get tossed overboard was our values. My ideal of Tom's of Maine as a values-centered company had backslid into pure bottom-line thinking.

I tried to rally management, erase the turf battles between departments, and wipe out politics altogether. By the end of the year, Kate, the board, and I agreed that we needed to ask some people to leave the company. It was a wrenching decision because these were good people, some of whom had made big sacrifices to join the company. But not everyone is suited for Managing Upside Down. To fill the gaps in marketing and sales, we had to pull junior people from the bench. Kate continued to push for new product development, and I left manufacturing and finance up to my financial partner Chet Homer so that I could hit the road to rebuild relationships with key customers, trying to boost sales, which had fallen from $17 to $15 million. Slowly, over the next few years, we started to bring back the business to pre-recall levels.

Getting Tom's of Maine back on the fast track was hard work, and it took its toll on Kate and me. After more than a quarter century of building a business, with four kids out of the house and our youngest about to head off to boarding school, we began to wonder whether we really wanted to be spending our lives trying to convince our own business executives to be as committed to the company's values as we were.

This question was on our minds in 1996 when we convened a family meeting with Pearl Rutledge, a psychologist who has sat on our board since the 1980s and who had been meeting with us periodically to explore the children's interest in the family business. With Kate and me exhausted, the nest emptying, and the kids trying to figure out what to do with their own lives, we decided to put two issues on the dining room table: (1) What were our talents and gifts, and how did we want to use them in the future? (2) How did Tom's of Maine fit into these personal profiles, and what was our responsibility to the company?

The children said that Tom's of Maine was extremely important to them and that they would like to help the company and even work part-time for it; but each also isolated a primary talent that was likely to move them in directions away from the company. Our eldest son, Chris, was a talented musician and composer who had moved to Seattle after college, where he was working part-time with our regional sales people to support his music. Matt had also gone west after college, to work as a chef, but eventually tired of the late-night lifestyle and returned home to join Tom's of Maine. But he was considering going to graduate school and had plans to start his own business, a kind of retreat for executives that would help them connect to the world of nature. Sarah had recently graduated from college and, after a stint working for one nonprofit in San Francisco and another in Idaho, had also returned to Maine for some business experience in the family company; but she, too, was already finetuning a business plan for a nonprofit therapeutic riding organization that she wanted to start with her new husband. Eliza was about to graduate from college and also had plans for her own clothing design business. We were proud of them all and truly amazed by their business ambitions. (Even our youngest, Luke, whose main concern was high school, had shown evidence of his entrepreneurial genes by starting—at thirteen—an ambitious bagel business on the island where we spend our August vacation.)

It was not surprising to Kate and me that Tom's of Maine was not our children's top priority. During the past few years, Kate, too, had been carving out more time away from the company for her art and poetry. She was showing her paintings at local galleries, had several poems published in various literary journals, and was in the midst of teaching a literature course at Harvard under the tutelage of the well-known psychiatrist, teacher, and author Robert Coles. So her decision to cut loose altogether from the family business and devote herself full-time to her writing and art was also no big surprise.

The real shocker was that after some thought, I realized that Tom's of Maine, the primary focus of my entire life for almost three decades, came second on my own list. I wanted to spend more time writing and teaching and, as a forum for both, to develop an idea I had for a nonprofit organization—"The Saltwater Institute," I called it—dedicated to teaching corporate executives about values-centered leadership.

A couple of months later, after considerable discussion and personal agonizing, Kate and I sadly, reluctantly, but decisively announced to our board and then to our kids that we wanted to explore the possibility of selling Tom's of Maine. The children appeared to take this decision with equanimity, happy that we were slowing down and pursuing our passions. Sarah, however, later confided that after she heard the news from me on the phone, she stepped into the shower, grabbed her shampoo—the Tom's of Maine baby shampoo that she had been using since toddlerhood—and suddenly got very emotional. Eliza, echoing her brother Chris's longstanding jibe that the company was Tom and Kate's "sixth child," recalled that the news that the company was on the block felt like we were deciding to sell one of the kids. But they supported the decision, for Mom and Dad's sake, and also realized that the company was valuable enough so that in the end all the Chappells would gain a kind of financial freedom that would permit us to head in the directions we wanted to go.

REFOCUSING ON OUR VALUES

Working with the board of directors and the investment banking firm Brown Brothers Harriman & Co., Kate and I selected six companies that were global in size and would, in our opinion, continue to grow the company. In past years, several large companies had expressed interest in Tom's of Maine, but we had ruled out some of them because we knew they really didn't share the company's mission to respect people and the environment. We resisted putting them on our shortlist. From the outset, I warned the selection committee we had formed that there would be some dealbreakers, values that we considered at the core of Tom's of Maine that the buyers would have to embrace: (1) keeping the company in Maine, (2) retaining a reasonable number of employees, (3) sticking to our commitment to be "natural," and (4) no animal testing.

Over the next four months, two of the six companies that fit our bill of particulars emerged as the front-runners. Meantime, we kept our employees posted on what was going on in open company meetings. Needless to say, there was considerable concern: Would the company be moved from Maine, what about their job security, should they dare buy a house? We scheduled regular meetings to announce any substantive progress and listen to the fears and concerns of our employees. The one thing we held back, however, was our own nagging and deepening dread over what we were about to give away. It became increasingly clear that the buyers didn't want to make the product in Maine. They didn't need our marketing people or our management. Nor were they aligned with our standards of "natural" and our commitment to cruelty-free products. They wanted the trademark, they wanted Tom and Kate, and they wanted to benefit from the synergy of wrapping us into their factories and into their packaged goods strategy. They probably would have reduced our product line to the few items that worked best for them. Here were these giant companies who were looking for room in their portfolios for this thing called "Tom's of Maine." But what we saw as the core of Tom's of Maine—its values—would truly evaporate, leaving only toothpaste, deodorant, and a trademark. These values provided a complexity to Tom's of Maine that made a deal far too cumbersome for a global marketer.

Kate and I decided to terminate the formal exploration process of selling the company. We informed our children, the board, and the investment bankers, who were disappointed but philosophical. After all, from the outset, I had made it clear why I could not journey this far in life on the basis of my values, build a company on those values, and then suddenly toss them out the window—even for financial independence for me and my family. Kate and I had given the exploration process its due, but when all the cards were on the table, we did not like what we saw. We said, "This is not for us."

It was one of the biggest turning points of my life—and proof of a connection to something bigger than I, my family, my company, and the global giants that wanted to buy us. Goodness had intervened. Our life's work was about to be turned over for cash, and we realized that the company had become more than a profitable enterprise: Tom's of Maine was selling values as well as toothpaste, mouthwash, and other personal care products. We could not compromise our mission.

AND THREE YEARS LATER?

Kate and I have not had any second thoughts about that decision. Once we made it, we looked to the future, and today, a mere three and a half years into that future, the exploration process seems like ancient history. We rarely talk about it—until something occurs to remind us what an important decision it was, not just for our family and us but for all the people who work for Tom's of Maine.

The news shocked the entire company. The year 1999 had barely begun when we heard that Don Cole's eighteen-year-old son, Jake, had been killed. Don had worked for Tom's of Maine for more than twenty years in shipping and toothpaste production. He is a hardworking and valued employee whom I also consider a friend. As the high school junior was driving to school with his girlfriend on an icy back road, their car hit a patch of ice and swerved into an oncoming vehicle. Jake was killed instantly, and his girlfriend, who was driving, was critically injured. (The driver of the other car was also hurt.)

The wake and funeral were packed with friends showing their consolation and support for Don and his wife Shirley. Many of them were Tom's of Maine employees. After the funeral, Kate and I decided to drive over to the beach. Amidst Maine coast's stark, cold natural beauty that seemed the right antidote to the sadness we had just experienced, we talked and reflected and began to realize how different that weekend would have been if we had sold the company. How many of those consoling hands might not have been there? Kate and I realized that there were not just friends on hand, but a *community* of support, from everyone at Tom's of Maine. After almost three decades in Kennebunk, the company has been part of the whole adult lives of many of its employees. Kate and I know their wives and husbands; we have sweated out births and broken bones and watched their kids go from strollers through college and into adulthood.

During the services for young Jake Cole, that sense of community had become even larger and stronger to Kate and me because we knew how close we had come to scuttling it. This was not the first death in the Tom's of Maine community, of course, and the whole company has always responded with the same kind of love and compassion it showed for the Coles. But this time, Kate and I realized that it might have been otherwise—if the Chappells had sold out, thus breaking up the very community that had come out to help pull Don and Shirley through this tragedy.

As we talked at the beach about the past few days, as we began to realize how much the company meant to its employees and the area, Kate and I began to feel older, wiser, and more peaceful about our decision to hang in there. We had definitely made the right move. We were still working hard, and God knows we still have our debts. But the company we were building was deep, interconnected, and rich in ways where money seemed quite beside the point.

Once again, it was a matter of reorientation.

LET YOUR VALUES DRIVE YOUR COMPANY

Most businesses focus on their business plans and strategies: Where do we want to go? How do we get there? Our transformation at

Tom's of Maine began with first finding out who we were and what we believed in. Then, given those beliefs, those *values*—being socially and environmentally responsible as well as financially successful—we thought long and hard about what kind of difference we could make in the world. We started not with financial goals, but with what we valued. We had business strategies, but not until our goals meshed with our values. We began by wanting to serve people and the environment and figured out how to achieve that profitably. And when it came down to cashing in or continuing to serve the company mission, the values stated in that mission were so deeply imbedded in all of us that walking away from the pretty penny that those companies were willing to pay for Tom's of Maine was amazingly easy.

HOW CAN YOU GET VALUES AT THE CENTER OF YOUR BUSINESS?

First, you have to begin to look at your business upside down—that is, not only from your own management perspective, but from the point of view of your employees; not only from your view of increasing the market, but also from the point of view of your market, your customers. Instead of waking up in the morning with a jolt with market share, sales, return on investment, and how much you're worth running through your head, you want to also consider your responsibilities to other things that you hold sacred in this world, such as human dignity, your family, your community, and the future of the rivers, the land, and thc air around you.

Managing Upside Down is a constant balancing act. I like to compare it to heading down a river in a canoe or kayak, coursing a stream. Sometimes the channel of the river heads more toward the left bank; other times, the deep water follows the center of the river or the right bank. But the paddler is always mindful of both banks, looking for the rocks coming up on the left, watching out for that log sticking out on the right. Who would concentrate only on one bank? You're on the lookout for safe water. The route down the river is not simple. Neither is life, or business. In both, we must learn to keep all the variables in mind, to respond quickly to changes forced on you by other forces, to benefit from trial and error, and, above all, to balance objectives that at first seem contradictory.

In business, we are inclined to focus on only one bank: profit-making. I am asking you to shift away from that, to reorient your thinking, not to forget the bottom line, but, as you go down the river, to keep an eye on the opposite bank—on your values—and look for a route that respects the dangers (and the benefits) of both sides of the river. Don't let either your desire for profit or to do good sink you. Integrate them both into your daily business practices, and rest assured that by paying attention to your social responsibilities, profits can follow.

Buddhists speak of this as searching for ''the middle way.'' If you just flinched at the mention of something so unbusinesslike as Buddhism, that's good. We're talking about reorienting your whole take on business here, and that will require shaking up your current intuitions and expectations about business. Managing Upside Down is not American business in some kind of New Age disguise, nor is it political correctness. That's not what I'm after at all. I have in mind something much more revolutionary. I'm talking about reversing the values of American business by making social responsibility a prerequisite of being in business. Too many people in business, even those who in their personal lives are sensitive to social and environmental concerns, believe that such values have no place in the marketplace. They do. Every one of us has a moral obligation to serve our communities and protect our environment. And we do not give up that obligation, that ''stewardship,'' when we go into business. Being socially and environmentally sensitive, along with being profitable, is what you ought to want your business to be.

Traditionally, the American businessman has been portrayed as an alternative version of the frontiersman, a rugged individualist, a kind of Davy Crockett in the boardroom. I want to respect that individual, entrepreneurial drive, but I also want to harness it to a more egalitarian, democratic spirit. I want the CEO to stop looking in the mirror long enough to listen to what his employees might have to say.

THE SMART BOSS KNOWS HE CAN LEARN FROM HIS EMPLOYEES

Most managers assume that time is money. At Tom's of Maine, we've learned that losing some production time can actually increase your production. Increasing productivity requires getting employees to work harder. Simple. But how best to motivate your workers, with a carrot or a stick?

I suggest you ask them. To find out what our employees are thinking, Tom's of Maine has created "Time Out Sessions" once every five or six weeks for ninety minutes. Over coffee and pastries, we spend time together discussing our families, telling each other stories about what's going on in our lives. At Tom's of Maine we don't expect all our employees to be the same. In fact, for years we have striven for diversity. Our Time Out Sessions go a long way to helping all of us get beyond appearances—whether gender, skin color, religion, educational background, or my title of CEO.

We estimate that every hour we produce about $20,000 worth of product. So each Time Out can cost us $30,000 in lost production. Multiply that by eight or nine times a year and we're talking real money. But we reckon we make it back and then some as a result of the imagination, creativity, efficiency, and just plain hard work we get from employees delighted to work for a company that cares about them as individuals and family members. Creating a community builds trust among its members.

One topic of conversation that cuts across all job categories is that employees need more time with their families. You know the figures: Almost half the women in America are in the workforce. Two paychecks per family have become an economic necessity for millions of couples, particularly those with children. Working couples need employers who recognize what they're up against every day.

Three years ago, a group of my manufacturing people came to me with a proposition: "We would like to get out of here at noon on Fridays during the summer." To do so, they were willing to commit to packing their forty-hour production schedule into a shorter workweek. It was an intriguing idea, and quite understandable given our location. Tom's of Maine is headquartered in a historic and beautiful part of Maine with picture-postcard American homes, romantic harbors, scenic beaches, great lobster, and, thus, a zillion summer visitors. We also have long winters, and this group of employees was suggesting that for ten weeks of the year they would like to enjoy their hometown as much as the tourists.

It was hard to disagree. But what about the nonmanufacturing employees, who were not as tightly scheduled and whose work was not as easily quantifiable? Should we make this "Summer Friday" thing a company-wide policy? And what about our clients? After some research and discussion, we noted that things around the office tended to slow down on Fridays in the summer, nor was there a lot of business coming through the door. (Apparently our customers and clients were just as eager to get away for the weekend as we were.) So we decided that all of us would get off work early on Friday, and it has worked fine for three years now. It was a wonderful idea that came from the plant floor, we listened, we acted, everyone delivered, and Summer Fridays has been a success. People really look forward to those ten weeks. And by showing our flexibility and trust, we built even more trust among our employees. The work gets done, and people spend the weekend with their families.

Time, in business, is definitely money. But time can also be a gift. It takes a certain kind of leader to recognize the benefits of listening to employees—not to mention customers, retailers, local charities, and community leaders. The kind of people who get to the top of the American business world are smart, ambitious, and inclined to think that once they've made it to the top, they have learned everything they need to know during that upward climb. You know the kind of person I'm talking about. I certainly do—because I used to be that kind of CEO, full of pride, unwilling to listen to any ideas but my own.

That kind of leader has no place in a values-oriented organization. If you are serious about learning to Manage Upside Down, you will have to accept a new definition of leadership.

2

Leadership

Most companies are organized in the shape of a pyramid, with supreme power residing at the top. Creativity and innovation, too, are supposed to emerge from the big corner offices with the view. The CEO says, "This is the way it will be done," and his subordinates rush off to make it happen.

In Managing Upside Down, power flows in the opposite direction—from the market, customers, and employees. In a values-driven company, innovation can come from anywhere; indeed, the main responsibility of a values-oriented leader is to encourage new ideas to come from everywhere. "Superiors" and "subordinates" have no place in the creative process. The muses of creativity do not care about job titles. Two heads (or more) are always better than one. The wisdom of the group trumps the opinion of one individual. Any team of employees can brainstorm about a new product, marketing strategy, package design, or manufacturing procedure. In a values-oriented company, a leader's primary job is not to wield power, but to draw it from every member of the group.

If it seems as if I am asking you to embrace opposites—individuality and community—you're right. That's the point of Managing

Upside Down: contradictory positions, such as being both a strong leader and a collaborator, can live together; better still, the resulting tension can be extremely creative and productive.

To prove it, I invented "acorns."

POWER TO THE PEOPLE!

Once Kate and I decided not to sell the company, we had to look to the future, which was a very scary sight: There were no new products on the horizon. Tom's of Maine had not created a new product in thirty-six months. Product development seemed stymied: our fifteen-person interdepartmental product development group seemed more eager to come up with reasons not to develop new products. Kate, who headed up product development, and I spent hours at night talking about the inclination of our people to throw up hurdles to new ideas. We could not have had a better departmental mix; marketing, engineering, and science were all represented. The result, unfortunately, was more politics than products. Science wanted to control R&D; so did marketing, both for obvious reasons. Worse still, most of the people in this product development group, we realized, were either not conceptual thinkers or were just unwilling to take chances.

I decided to experiment with smaller, more flexible teams of no more than three people, each dedicated to generating new ideas for toothpaste, mouthwash, soap, and natural dental floss. I expected big things from these small groups, which I call acorns. The idea was first to come up with an idea for a new product, figure out if it was possible scientifically, and then see if there was a place for such a product in the marketplace by bouncing the new idea off our customers. That meant that each acorn would require a scientist on board, as well as someone to do consumer research. To avert political sniping, I decided to put at the head of each acorn a product "champion," not necessarily a member of the top management from any department, but someone imaginative enough to see an opportunity for a new product, encourage the others to play with the idea, and then make sure these new notions got tested.

I saw this champion as the antithesis of the classic business school model of the manager/analyst who examines the current market, factors in trends, and tries to figure out how to beat what's already out there in the market. The acorn leader would measure her idea not against the competition but against the company's objectives, which are driven not by the market but by the mission. The champion would be a leader who was a creative resource rather than a negative force.

But where would I find my champions? Executives in the interdepartmental product group seemed to cancel each other out with their narrow concerns for their own budgets, market trends, or the retailers' concerns about shelf space. I needed creative minds that were plugged into the company's values and able to think for themselves. Above all, in order to jump-start an entirely new R&D process, I needed people who were not afraid of me.

I turned to my family. My wife and co-founder, Kate, who also happens to be a professional artist and published poet, would head the mouthwash acorn; my eldest, Chris, a musician, would champion the dental floss group; Matt, the former chef, would take on the toothpaste acorn. For soap, I went outside the family to one of the more creative people in the company. Needless to say, the announcement of this new product development concept did not meet with a chorus of hosannas. The staff accepted the omnipresence of Chappells, of course, but their reluctance hung over the offices like a Maine fog.

Meantime, the acorns went to work. One of our earliest and most successful products was a baking soda toothpaste, much imitated by our competitors. Kate suggested a baking soda mouthwash. Immediately, scientific obstacles were thrown up: "You can't put baking soda into a mouthwash and expect it to remain baking soda," said the chemists. If the baking soda broke down, their argument went, you could not properly call the product a baking soda mouthwash. Our consumer research people, however, discovered that customers loved the idea of a baking soda natural mouthwash. Kate challenged the scientific group to prove that a genuine baking soda mouthwash could not be made. The chemists worked their magic and, lo and behold, the baking soda did not break down in the mouthwash, and thus we had a genuine baking soda mouthwash. We came up with flavors in peppermint and gingermint, went to market in January 1999, and at this writing the baking soda mouthwash was holding its own in the marketplace. In fact, if the gingermint keeps selling at its current pace, it might end up as our best-selling flavor of all time.

The champion of the dental floss acorn, Chris Chappell, pushed for a natural floss. We had been using a nylon fiber that included natural waxes and natural bioflavanoids. Chris insisted that Tom's of Maine ought to have a floss that was more than sort of natural. He was informed that the idea of a genuinely natural floss had been raised years ago, but was quickly ditched because a natural fiber did not exist on the market. "Let's find out how to make one," said Chris, who then set out to examine whether such natural sources as linen, hemp, or silk could do the trick. The acorn ran the natural floss idea past the consumers, who were enthusiastic. Eventually, Chris discovered a research center at the University of North Carolina that is a leader in floss research. Several months later, we had a prototype made from each of these raw materials.

The toothpaste acorn, championed by my son Matt, has generated four new flavors of children's toothpaste as well as a product for sensitive teeth. Kate's mouthwash acorn generated the baking soda mouthwash; she also had the idea for the gingermint flavor that is flying out of the stores. The soap acorn, after faltering in its initial efforts to create a liquid soap, has now put on the market four new Tom's of Maine liquid soaps.

Before the advent of the acorns, we had gone almost three years without creating a new product: in less than eighteen months, the new acorns slammed out twenty-six new personal care products. We then created three more acorns relating to a new business concept in natural wellness. I myself championed the cough and cold acorn and asked Chris to champion new herbal supplements. Once we decided to go ahead with this new wellness business, within eighteen months of that green light, we had seventy-five more products—a 300 percent increase. If Kate and I had announced to our old fifteen-person interdepartmental product development group that our goal over the next two years was one hundred new products, they would have called for the straightjackets.

I had proved that we could create radical ideas for new products by giving people permission to think and act creatively. By setting up small, autonomous product development groups, championed by someone passionate about a new idea who can also restrain the group from slipping into negative thinking and keep them focused on their product vision, you can generate new products. It's the concept that drives the process, numbers be damned, technology be damned, science be damned. The only ally the champion with a new product idea needs is a group of consumers who want that product.

Thus, in two years we have increased our number of products from twenty-seven to 117! That's not just progress, that's *transformation*!

BUT WHO IS THE ULTIMATE LEADER?

The company's values. One of the reasons the acorn idea can be so effective in a values-driven company like Tom's of Maine is that the ultimate goal of any product is never in doubt. It must be natural, it must be in line with the company's mission of social and environmental responsibility, and it must be good.

In Managing Upside Down, the CEO is not at the center of the enterprise. Our beliefs and mission are. (And so is our "Reason for Being," a third statement we have drafted that I'll discuss in Chapter 5.) In a values-oriented company, top management plays a larger role not because of their power, but by virtue of their authority. As the founding CEO of Tom's of Maine who also owns the controlling interest of the company, I certainly hold both power and authority. In the values-oriented company, authority and power are not synonyms. In this collaborative, participatory form of doing business, power—to innovate, to create, to criticize, and to solve—is shared by everyone. *Authority,* on the other hand, must still remain in the hands of certain designated people who are in a position to allocate resources to the group and ultimately hold the responsibility to say yes or no or go back to the drawing board. While the traditional CEO feeds off his obvious ability to succeed (he made it to CEO, didn't he?) and his infallible decision-making skills, the values-oriented leader understands his own fallibility and thus prefers to bank on the wisdom of the group. The Upside Down Manager recognizes that creativity may emerge from the unlikeliest places. Guidance comes from a set of rules called your values, which are available to every member of the enterprise, no matter what their job title might be. A values-oriented leader uses his authority to unleash the creative power of his people.

I have come to recognize the benefits—indeed, the genius—of sharing power instead of throwing it around. My biggest creative resource, I have come to appreciate, is our people. Give your employees permission to be creative, regardless of their job description, and watch out!

FLATTENING THE HIERARCHY

At Tom's of Maine, we have discarded the idea of "superior" versus "subordinate." To escape the restraints of hierarchy, we have toppled the traditional pyramid of power, junking such titles as vice president of this and that, which tend to concentrate power at the top of the company, inspiring fear among those on the lower rungs of the organizational chart. We have toppled the old hierarchy into equal "groups" headed not by vice presidents but by "group team leaders" (e.g., group team leader of finance and information technology, of consumer and brand development, of new product development, of customer business development).

The best business executives are bound to be ambitious. If there is a mountain in view, they will try to climb it. We've decided to flatten the terrain in our company so that the only thing worth conquering is our business objectives. Dispensing with the built-in superiority of traditional corporate titles, our job descriptions have substituted more collegial labels that reflect our new, more collaborative system of governance. Those in charge of various teams, initiatives, and projects are called "leaders," and their role is to "supervise," "sponsor," "coach," and "support."

The boss of bosses at Tom's of Maine is the company's mission, which stands at the center of our new organization. All the departments—sales, marketing, new product development, manufacturing, science—have been reconstituted into teams that work simultaneously, independent yet interconnected, the tension spread equally, but splaying out from the mission in a web of functions. The circle represents inclusiveness in the group, open dialogue between its members, encouraging everyone's participation, their ideas, and their passion. We are big on circles at Tom's of Maine—the "talking circle," something we borrowed from Native American culture, where the circle is the basis of ritual gatherings, representing the idea that everything is connected to everything else. I have adapted the talking circle to our business as a way to improve our ability to listen to one another and solve problems together, no matter what our position in the company or our backgrounds. The power of the circle is its openness. It makes someone's idea the group's idea. When you confer in a circle, no one is left out. It's amazing how a small group of people talking can become a force that can transform the morale—and the creativity—of a company.

But every circle must have a triangle, which stands for leadership in the context of diversity. Everyone occupies one of these triangles. Some have more responsibility and thus authority than others do;

they will be held more accountable for parts of the business. That is a reality. Group efforts need someone with the authority to make decisions, organize efforts, and allocate resources. And so there is a head to every team, every department, and every committee.

Finally, we are all agents of the mission. Everyone's individual relative role within that mission and how we all interrelate has to be absolutely clear. Each job description is explicit about what a job's responsibilities are, along with the employee's key relationships within a given group. In the end, our employees are accountable to four things: (1) the company's statements of beliefs, mission, and reason; (2) their teams; (3) their immediate team leader; and (4) their own personal growth. Only with these things spelled out can there be reasonable expectations of what people should be doing and how they should be held accountable. We have been working hard at this kind of operational thinking, whose goal is to get the roles we play, the work we do, and the business plans we make to be responsible to the company's values.

Leadership is a process, not a person. It is a mechanism for teaching, coaching, and facilitating others to come up with new ideas that are in line with the company's core values. The group might easily head down a wrong road, stray from its values. It is the leader's job to refocus them, to remind them of their goal, their destination. The CEO's job is to stimulate that creativity, encourage it, and act as a kind of midwife for the best ideas. The values-oriented leader is just another part of this process of collaboration, a member in this partnership and dialogue.

Collaborative leaders play the following roles in their organizations:

- Keep the organization's values paramount at all times.
- Form groups—on a standing or ad hoc basis—with diverse and complex membership capable of dealing with the assigned task.
- Provide the resources—research, time, money—that will allow the group to do its job as well as possible.
- Coach, facilitate, nurture, affirm, question, and support the group as it strives toward its objective.
- See that the work assigned to the group and the recommendations of the group are considered in a timely fashion, and only after trying to summon the creative power of each member of the group.
- Never be afraid to make a mistake. The healthy organization will learn from that error, adjust, and make better decisions in the future.

We have turned our departments upside down; we have broken down the hierarchy. If a twenty-seven-year-old has a great idea and makes it happen, great. What is at the center of the company is not experience, nor politics, nor the budget, nor power. Our only master is the mission. The goal is for every move, every business strategy, to be driven by not the market but what we believe in. We care about formulating our products with natural ingredients; we care about treating our employees fairly and decently; we care about families, neighborhoods, communities, and the natural world. Our job is to *serve* all those constituencies.

But that kind of leadership takes more than pinning your values on the wall like slogans in a locker room. The company mission cannot be a list of don'ts, like some corporate Ten Commandments. Once you put your finger on the things you care most about in your life and your work—your values—you have to live them and breathe them. Lip service will not do. I have learned that the hard way. And so will you, unless you put your values at the center of your business strategies and stick to them without compromise.

THE KEY TO MANAGING UPSIDE DOWN: INTENTIONALITY

Recently we were in the final stages of buying a small herbal extraction company in Vermont. We had an agreement in concept that the owner would make the extracts we needed in large quantities and send them to us in Maine in fifty-five-gallon drums. I asked our finance, engineering, and manufacturing people to visit the Vermont facility to see how we could update the operation, which had previously handled much smaller quantities than we required.

Once they got there and checked out the possibilities, they suddenly got excited about moving our entire new herbal and natural medicinal business to Vermont. For a few days this prospect caught me off guard. I was buying into the idea, though it seemed pretty radical. The company had long been committed to the communities of Kennebunk and Maine. We had been talking about putting our entire operation—R&D, manufacturing, executive offices, child care, even new facilities open to the local community—on a new "campus" on property in Kennebunk that we already owned. Now this team was recommending splitting off the newest part of the business and relocating it in Vermont, and I'm committed to teamwork, so I didn't rule it out. I asked the same team to do a comparative analysis of doing it all in Vermont versus extraction in Vermont and added value packaging in Maine, as I had first suggested. The figures came back: Splitting the job between Vermont and Maine would cost us an extra $250,000 in equipment and supervisory personnel.

I was committed to Maine. We were Tom's of Maine, after all. The plans to expand in the town of Kennebunk were also important to the company's values and to the town. We decided to go against the normal business instinct to calculate the lowest cost approach. Instead, we opted for spending more money now on spreading the work between Maine and Vermont. And thus we honored our values as well as the jobs in the Vermont plant. We also began discussing what it would take to move a growing factory from Vermont to Maine three years down the line.

Without a clear mission, without our commitment to Maine and

Kennebunk, this decision would not have happened. We would have followed the arithmetic. Commitment to your values, neverending vigilance, constant sensitivity—what I call "intentionality"—is the key to Managing Upside Down. For most of us, this requires not only a reorientation from profit to values, but is a radical change of behavior. You have to change your habits, from self-interest to serving others. You will have to transform the culture of your company. Instead of being driven by outside forces, such as the market, demographics, and the numbers, you have to pay attention to what moves you from the inside. Your values have to be at the center of who you really are. Once you have a mission, you cannot let anything get in its way.

Even your budget. Particularly your budget. We sell our toothpaste in the classic aluminum tube, the kind that most of us remember from our childhood, squeezed all over or carefully rolled up from the bottom, depending on your personality. If you hadn't noticed, everyone else in the toothpaste business uses plastic tubes. Why? Plastic cuts costs and increases your profits. End of argument, at least in any business where profit is king. At Tom's of Maine, the issue is never that simple because profit is not our only standard of measurement of what's good for our company. We have our beliefs and mission statements that commit us to protecting the environment, and to that end, aluminum tubes are a better choice for us: they oxidize in landfills, while plastic never decays. Aluminum can also be recycled, which we encourage our customers to do with their used Tom's of Maine toothpaste tubes. The debate over plastic versus aluminum has been long and hard. Several years ago, our marketing director commissioned compatibility studies of various kinds of plastic tubes. I stopped her because no form of plastic could fit with our commitment to the environment. And that seemed to be that.

Until recently, that is, when the plastic versus aluminum controversy was raised again—this time on environmental grounds. It takes a great deal of extra energy to create an aluminum tube. Thus, while we have a recyclable product that won't sit in landfills for eternity, we are also using up another valuable resource—electricity—by going with aluminum. After considerable debate and cost analysis (aluminum adds 10 percent to our costs), we have decided to stick with the aluminum. But we also decided to enlarge our recycle symbol on the tubes to encourage customers not to toss them into the garbage. We're also talking to regional recyclers to help us increase toothpaste tube recycling.

That's the revolutionary part of Managing Upside Down. Every decision you make, every business plan you write has to live up to this mission. It is not about choosing—sometimes your values, sometimes the bottom line. Managing Upside Down eliminates that dichotomy by integrating the pursuit of values with the pursuit of profit. At Tom's of Maine, the only master we all are obliged to serve is the mission.

Warning: Not everyone you hire will get that.

MANAGING UPSIDE DOWN REQUIRES VALUES-SENSITIVE MANAGERS

Once my board and I had committed Tom's of Maine to social responsibility, I believed all I had to do was hire professional managers eager to work in a values-oriented company and then hand them copies of the mission and belief statements. Boy, was I wrong. I had no idea how difficult it would be for people to come from large American corporations like Gillette or Colgate and live the Tom's of Maine mission. (And neither did they.) It was too different from the corporate cultures they had grown up in, too upside down. No matter how much they might say they were committed to the company's values, no matter how much they might tell themselves they were committed to the mission, when it came down to day-to-day business, they were inclined to replay the techniques and tools they had learned at their old companies, remaining slavishly accountable to their departmental budgets. We would concoct a plan and take it on the road. Enthusiasm was high. But if we fell short thirty days or sixty days, the budgeteers would jump right in with their long knives, cutting someone's budget to protect the bottom line. There was a genuine fear of spending money.

It may seem an odd thing for a boss to complain about, not spending enough money. But remember, I am an entrepreneur, and the one thing I learned quickly in my career trying to make something from nothing is that if you don't spend some cash, you will not get any results. When you tighten the purse strings, you also put the squeeze on everyone's potential, squelching their ideas. I could see a physical change take place among my employees: shoulders went round, heads bowed to the ground, and people seemed to arrive in the office already defeated before the day began. Worse, when things got dicey at the bottom line, the first thing my managers were inclined to throw overboard to save money were the values: Suddenly, certain kinds of recyclable products might be too expensive, and the outserts we included in our packaging to explain the Tom's of Maine mission or to tell stories about how we donated money to environmental causes disappeared. At first I resisted. But their fear became contagious. They waved the gloomy projections in my face, pointed to the necessary cuts, and I demurred. They wore me down. It was more than frustrating because there I was, committed to the company's values, allowing those values to be compromised. I began to question whether it was really possible to create a company that was truly values-centered.

And then I realized that my problem was hardly that profound: I had just hired the wrong people. They were good people, talented, experienced. I considered them my friends. We just couldn't figure out how to work together. I knew they were the wrong people because I hadn't chosen *all* the wrong people. At the top of my company, in certain departments, I had executives as committed to the mission as I. They delivered, and I stayed the hell out of their way. The second bit of evidence that the kind of managers I was looking for actually existed was my own kids. Four of my children are now working at Tom's of Maine. They had to learn the ropes: each of them found a niche inside various departments and learned their jobs;

each of them dealt with the initial (and understandable) resentment about being the boss's kid and then succeeded well enough to turn their critics into fans. What my children did not have to learn was the company's values. They had grown up on them. Caring about people and the environment was, literally, mother's milk to them.

I realized that if these young people could live and breathe the values of the company, then so could other young executives. I just had to find them. What I needed were people who already exhibited a commitment to others, their community, and the environment. One of my earliest advisors, and a member of my board since 1980, John Rockwell, who had been the senior vice president and director of Booz Allen & Hamilton, the New York consulting firm, said to me, "You need to find competent executives you can trust and empower. I give you permission to make mistakes finding those people."

What an incredible thing to say: You can make some mistakes.

LOOKING FOR A NEEDLE IN A STACK OF NEEDLES

As soon as Kate and I announced to the investment bankers that we were no longer interested in selling the company, we switched to Plan B: finding a chief operating officer who would help us grow Tom's of Maine under the Chappell family ownership, according to the company's mission. This person would not just work for me or be my right-hand man; he would be a true partner, someone willing to Manage Upside Down. My kids seemed relieved. Since then, however, I have learned that though they were happy that Tom's of Maine was staying in the family, they were skeptical about whether Dad could really give up the reins and share power.

What they failed to take into account was that as a family, we had let our values show us the way. Perhaps, too, my kids had no idea how strong my own commitment to collaboration had become. After the management crisis of the past few years, I was eager to wipe out the turf battles inside the company; the political infighting had to be controlled. I had already begun to think of ways to flatten the traditional corporate hierarchy and spread power throughout the company. I was convinced that the right COO could help me further alter the management structure of Tom's of Maine.

Of course, we were looking for a needle in a haystack: A top executive in the packaged goods business who had run a company or at least a big chunk of one, who had to be committed to managing by values; more important, not only did this person have to be compatible with me and my entrepreneurial style, the perfect COO had to be good at the very things I wasn't. "What you need, Tom," John Rockwell kept saying to me, "is someone who can partner with you intellectually and commercially, and then at the end of the day can go back to the office and build this company." Rock kept telling me that the dream partner for me would be a second-generation founder, a person who could take an entrepreneur's company and turn it into an entrepreneurial company.

That became my dream, too. My family, I later found out, considered it an impossible dream. They doubted whether I could find such a committed person to the Tom's of Maine mission outside my own family and the small circle of executives who had been with the company for years. I was also aware of the office scuttlebutt that I was so wrapped up with marketing, sales, and R&D that no one on God's green earth could satisfy me. I did not think that was true. There were people out there who could be my partners. I just hadn't found them.

I set out to find my COO and, after some stops and starts and a little miracle (which I will tell you about in the next chapter), I found Tom O'Brien. He was thirty-four years old, a Harvard MBA, and a homegrown star at Procter & Gamble, where he was running their worldwide men's deodorant division, an $850 million business. But he was antsy and looking for the meaning of it all. (Sound familiar?) Tom had even been searching for a company to buy that he could grow in line with his own ideas about corporate and social responsibility. He had done his homework on Tom's of Maine and was intrigued by the company's reputation for values. When he visited us in Maine and found that Kate's and my commitment to those values was unwavering and that our products were based on those values, he saw an opportunity (and a challenge) to build a much bigger company on the foundation Kate and I had created. He, too, wanted to build a company that was good for society. In short, that Tom was just what this Tom was looking for.

The first time we met, he brought with him two packages of Tom's of Maine deodorant that he had bought off the shelves in a local store. One had what we call an "outsert" on which we talk to our customers about what the company is up to, the other didn't. "Which is your current package?" he asked. I pointed to the one without the outsert. He said that bothered him because he had read the company mission "to include full and honest dialogue . . . about products and issues." Chagrined, I explained that according to my marketing people, the outsert packaging was just too expensive. Tom countered that putting a package on the shelves without the outsert was unacceptable if I was serious about the company's mission of communicating with the customer. He also pointed out that a decision so central to the mission should not be the marketing department's call. Why? He argued that the outsert expense should not be part of the marketing budget but part of the cost of the goods. "As far as I'm concerned, after reading your mission," he said, "if you don't look at communication with your customers as an ingredient, you and I see this mission differently. The insert/outsert is part of the product. Without it, you are just a toothpaste company or another personal care product company, albeit one committed to natural products. But if you're about social responsibility and if you want to encourage environmental sustainability, you have to have this information in your packaging." He made it very clear that if we were moving away from our dialogue with our customers on the packaging, then we didn't have anything to talk about it. I realized he was right, and I wrote to him thanking him for helping us get back on track.

Seven months after we had closed the door on selling the company, Tom O'Brien was sitting across the hall from me in our Kennebunk offices as my new COO. We had found a needle in a haystack. When Tom O'Brien came through the door, I suspect many of my executives heaved a sigh of relief. The boss had let a fox into the henhouse: a Harvard MBA, a P&G star, young; in short, one of them. Boy, were they wrong. It turned out that Tom O (as he is known around the office) would out-Tom Tom Chappell. The first thing he asked the managers was how the insert/outsert program was coming. They replied that it was too expensive and they weren't going to do it. Mystified, Tom explained that he had received a letter from me to the contrary. They acknowledged that I wanted it done, but conceded that they couldn't figure out a way to do it. "It is too expensive," was their reply. Tom immediately called a meeting of the products and marketing people and essentially said shipping a product out of this company without a message from Tom's of Maine was like sending out a bar of soap without a fragrance or toothpaste without calcium carbonate, the essential ingredient of toothpaste. "This is not negotiable," he said, adding that we had four months to get things right. Four months later, outserts were on our deodorant packaging, budgeted as an ingredient.

My point is that managing by values is a constant struggle, even in a company as committed to its mission as Tom's of Maine. It is never simple. One solution can create another problem. A valiant attempt to stick to one of your values can push you up against another of your values. Not long after dealing with the insert dilemma, Tom O'Brien discovered that we were sending out soap without an insert because he had ordered that the plastic packaging around our soap be discontinued, even though the plastic container was biodegradable and thus recyclable, making it cost efficient. Tom argued that if we were serious about sustaining the environment, then we ought to ditch this excess plastic packaging. He also argued that the plastic kept the consumer from smelling the product. But getting rid of one problem caused another. He had already made it clear that no product would go out of the company without an outsert or insert. Trouble was, the insert in the soap got moldy without the plastic between the paper and the soap. "Put an outsert on the package,"

Tom said. "Too expensive," came the reply. Once again, Tom had to explain that without this communication to the customer, you do not have a Tom's of Maine product.

So, with Tom O'Brien's help, we have redefined what a Tom's of Maine product actually is: Not only is it natural, but it also talks to the customers and invites them to talk back to the company. We are now learning that our insert/outsert program is probably one of the most significant things we did in 1997. Our retail customers love it. The health food trade, which began to think the company had abandoned its dialogue with customers when it went mass market, loves it. Our consumers are responding by mail in double the numbers over the previous year.

What's making all this work is our renewed commitment to Managing Upside Down. With Tom O'Brien's fresh take on how much values has become another product of Tom's of Maine, we all have become more committed to our mission, more intentional.

It was Tom O'Brien who also insisted that we had committed the company to growing in Kennebunk in a campus setting that would increase a sense of community for all our employees. Moving a chunk of the business to Vermont, he argued, would run counter to what we valued and believe in. I agreed.

THE NEXT STEP IS SEVEN STEPS

My own hiring failures have taught me that not every executive, no matter how smart or experienced, is capable of Managing Upside Down. Today, candidates for management positions at Tom's of Maine have to live and breathe social interest. A recruiting firm whose experience has been mainly in the worlds of education and not-for-profit organizations has helped us. This company understood that while we were looking for candidates with the right professional skills and experiences, values came first. It was their job to make sure the people they were sending us had a strong orientation to values, not just as a line item on their résumés but as part of their personality and upbringing. When I interview job candidates, I talk to them about their personal lives first. I like to move from our common interests as persons to a discussion between two professionals. That is our new employment model: Find young managers who care about the same things the company cares about, train them to make those values part of their very being and management style, and within six months, they're off and running.

To that end, I have devised the Seven Intentions, a practical guide for teaching executives how to become values-centered leaders. Each of these steps is designed to change you and your business. The Seven Intentions are a process, a journey to values-centered leadership, and I have tried to illustrate this process with our experiences at Tom's of Maine, both good and bad, to turn ourselves into a values-driven company. If you're still unsure whether you're up to the task of Managing Upside Down, take comfort in the fact that my company is still a work in progress. (And so am I.) We are trying to create a new way of doing business. The results so far, I am happy to say, have been so positive that I want to pass along what we have learned.

It is time to take the first step toward mastering Managing Upside Down.

3

Connect

INTENTION #1
Set aside your own ego, open up, and *connect* to an outside, universal force that is bigger than you and available to everyone, the power of goodness.

For me, the biggest obstacle to creating a values-centered company has been—me. It's taken me a long time to admit that in public. After all, you don't become an entrepreneur or a successful CEO without having a large, armor-plated ego and a tendency to swagger through the corridors. If your company is making magic out there in the marketplace, who doesn't begin to think he's Houdini?

Of course, I haven't created a successful company by myself. No one does. It just seems that way because so many of the decisions you make building a company are do-or-die ones. I've had all kinds of help, particularly from my co-founder and wife, Kate. But it has taken me almost thirty years, a great marriage, five kids, unimagined success, and some periods of equally inconceivable misery to come to terms with the virtue of humility. Every day, I still have to struggle to set aside my own ego and pride. For me, nothing has been tougher than learning to share power—the key to values-centered leadership.

How do you learn humility? By recognizing that there is something outside of you, a power beyond your self-interest, a force bigger than you—and then *connecting* to it. "Connect" is the first intention, the first step toward values-centered leadership. If you cannot take this step, you will not be able to master Managing Upside Down.

You probably think you're already way ahead of me: that this force, this power I am referring to is God. And if you yourself are not a religious person, you're figuring that there is no way that you will be able to learn this values-centered approach to management if it requires "finding God." Hang on. That's not what I'm saying at all.

In fact, I myself am a good example of how you can connect *without* religion.

THE WORST OF TIMES

During most of my business career, I kept a strong separation between church and commerce. Sure, I saw myself as a family man, committed to my community and the natural environment. I went to church on Sunday, gave to charity, was kind to animals. But, dammit, I was an entrepreneur/CEO, and five days a week I was as self-interested and full of pride as any CEO in America. When another's opinion went counter to mine, I ignored it. I made unilateral decisions about family vacations, and at work I sometimes made changes so fast that my own managers had no idea why we were making those changes. I would not even listen to an opposing view. Yet if anyone had dared confront me, I would have insisted that I was a collaborative person.

I remember one time looking out the window and seeing a young employee careen down the street and squeal into the parking lot. Presuming he was on drugs, I rushed out of my office, flew down the stairs, and met the culprit at the door. I pointed my finger at the road and told him he was out of here. No rational discussion, that was it. "Get the hell out!" Of course, I had no proof that he was on drugs (though it turned out I was right). But that's the way I behaved in those days: I was determined to have my own way, justified or not. That kind of manipulative, controlling, obsessive behavior feeds on itself, so that you tend to attract like-minded people. Soon everyone is wheeling and dealing, carving out their turf, playing politics. The result is an atmosphere poisoned by control and fear. Looking back, I now realize that the way I rationalized my behavior was by turning myself into two people, one very quick to judge and act, the other quite kind and generous. If someone criticized me for being harsh, I would calmly point to a long list of my magnanimous acts.

And then I hit a wall. I discovered that a close member of my family was exhibiting addictive behavior, and nothing I did or said or wanted to do could help. As I tried to figure out why, I came to realize that I had been exhibiting that same kind of addictive behavior day in and day out.

I had a drinking problem. And I had never acknowledged it because egotists like me do not admit to any problem, certainly any problem they could not solve. I had smarts, I had money, I had political influence, and I had the power of persuasion. And then one day, none of the above worked. I could not help a person I loved. I found myself utterly powerless.

That sense of powerlessness brought me literally to my knees, praying for help. It was an amazing experience. The one time in my life I could not control things, I saw my own brokenness. I realized that I had isolated myself from loved ones and colleagues because of my obsessions. Worse (because, remember, I was still a defensive know-it-all), I suddenly realized that my family had seen through me, and so had my colleagues. I had been difficult to work with, to live with, and all the while, I was thinking I was a prince of a human being. I had all the trimmings—the fancy education, the growing company, the big house, the boat—but I recognized that I was empty inside.

I also realized that I was risking losing everything I valued. This was a huge breakthrough for me. If I was going to help anyone else, particularly my loved ones, if I was going to be a true model for my family and for my employees, I needed to change. Now that I could point the finger at the real culprit—me—I could take another, more honest look at who I was and figure out how I might change. I also knew that the person who had screwed things up was not the one to look to for help. So I reached out. Soon I began to spend time with others who were recovering from their own drinking problems. I learned about my obsession by hearing about theirs and how they had overcome it. It was here, in the midst of this personal struggle, that I began to learn to turn my trust over to a higher power.

It was my vulnerability that had opened me to what I think of now as a spiritual experience, not my religious beliefs. Of course, as someone who had been raised in a religious family, I had a set of values, including the notion that helping others was better than just helping yourself. Unfortunately, I was too caught up with growing my company to pay much more than lip service to those values— until I hit that wall of powerlessness which opened me up to my spiritual side. Only when I was brought to my knees did I realize it was not such a bad place to start the day, expressing humility, affirming that the center of life was not Tom Chappell but something much larger. Only when I needed help did I realize that such help is always there. That is the power of goodness in the world. To connect to goodness, you have to eradicate what I call the "disease of self-centeredness."

I began to reevaluate my life and my work. As my values loomed larger in my life, I became frustrated that they were not more evident in my work. That was when I began to question whether I wanted to continue in the business world, retreating to divinity school where, to my surprise, I realized I could combine my talents as an entrepreneur/CEO with my urge to do good. I could be a capitalist *and* a moralist. And though my business, Tom's of Maine, was a private company, I began to see it as not just a money-making machine, but also as an entity in relation to other entities—employees, financial partners, customers, suppliers, even the earth itself.

And thus the beginning of my journey to change my company, to turn it upside down. I started connecting my company to goodness, letting universal values drive Tom's of Maine, not just the bottom line.

THE COMMON EXPERIENCE OF GOODNESS

What do I mean by goodness? Everyone has experienced a version of goodness, and you don't have to be pushed to the wall, like me, to find it: When you enjoy a work of art, thrill to a piece of music, feel that tingle in your spine when you read a passage in a novel, or (maybe even closer to home) feel the excitement that comes with a great business idea or the sudden, clear vision of a new product that never occurred to you before, you sense that you have been touched by something outside yourself. Remember when you fell in love? When things of this world grab you like this, in a way that we are inclined to think of as "deep," then you have been touched by goodness. This is what a spiritual experience is.

Notice that I am not saying that spirituality or goodness sits on some mountaintop, pulling our strings like some grand puppeteer. On the contrary, goodness is a part of our world, all around us, a kind of spiritual energy that brushes you like the wind. For centuries, thinkers have helped us understand such notions through words and images. Buddhists speak of the "Buddha nature within us," what the Greek philosopher Plato, who predates Christianity by more than three hundred years, called "the higher part of our soul." This is another way of saying that we humans have the ability to tap into something bigger and better than we are. For Plato, the virtuous man, the moral man, the "good man" had to be in contact with, to know—indeed, be *connected* to—certain moral absolutes such as beauty, courage, and virtue. He called these moral ideals "forms." But the dominant form for Plato, the virtue without which the others could not exist, was goodness.

To embrace the power of goodness is to push self-interest aside and to open yourself willingly. The good person acknowledges that not only does he live among other people, he must also respect them. Morality is a social relationship. "One alone is nothing," wrote the legendary eighteenth-century New England preacher Jonathan Edwards, who believed that individuals are shaped by their relation to others. Too many CEOs, I am convinced, believe that they stand above all others. I have played that game. Now I am content to admit to my imperfections and be a productive partner with my fellow workers, listen to their ideas with the enthusiasm I used to have only for my own. Ten years ago, my executives sought me out for political advantage; today, my co-workers (and sometimes members of their families) knock on my door and ask for my "wisdom."

Is this power of goodness God? For me, it is. Powerless, I reached out for help; I prayed to my God, and soon I was climbing out of that impasse in ways that defied logical explanation. But veering out of control, finding yourself vulnerable, and then reaching out for help is hardly an experience unique to religious people. Understanding that you are not alone in the world, that you have friends and family to depend on, that fellow workers can help you toward your goals, is a universal *human* experience. It is also one definition of morality, which, after all, is about how people deal with one another. And while you certainly can be a good person without being a religious person, I would argue that you couldn't be either and be a selfish person. So maybe in our secular world, it is here—in the common human experience of goodness—where morality and religion overlap.

It is also no place for an egotist. In fact, in the religious and metaphysical systems of the East *and* the West, since the beginning of history, finding what is true or good or perfect or moral or spiritual or God—whatever you call that independent, large force in the world—has required shedding egoism.

In my opinion (and experience), you cannot be a truly good business leader, either, without this kind of humility and respect for others. But once you open to goodness, it will be there for you when you need it.

GOODNESS DELIVERS

When I set out to find a partner for myself, my new COO, I tried to do it as systematically and objectively as possible. I chose a head-hunting firm that specialized in working with nonprofit organizations, which quickly came up with several pretty impressive candidates. Each visited the company and met with me, my wife, and my children. One man stood out, a head of a division of a multibillion-dollar company I have a lot of respect for. At forty-eight, he was interested in a quality-of-life change, professionally as well as personally. He had all the management credentials as well as the intellectual depth I thought this assignment required. The interviews went well, and then, as we were parting, he said, "I know you want to run R&D, but I would hope that within two years you would want me to run that."

Instantly, my enthusiasm for this person fell through the floor. When we had described this position, I had made it very clear that the one thing I definitely wanted to continue running at Tom's of Maine was R&D. "How did the interview go?" the recruiter asked. "Great," I said, " but he shot himself in the foot at the end of the day. I'm not interested in any more conversation." The recruiter was incredulous, crushed. But my mind was made up: I had made it clear from the start that I wanted to be active in contributing to the company's future, and I certainly did not want to bring in a partner who wanted to move me out of the one thing about Tom's of Maine that I was most passionate about.

It looked as though the skeptics, including members of my own family, were right: I wouldn't be able to find the miracle partner. But I refused to give up. I had discovered long ago that when you are connected to goodness, miracles can happen. In the midst of this recruitment process, another name had come up. I was in New York City doing some pro bono work for the General Theological Seminary, trying to teach a group of Episcopal bishops how to become more values-centered in running their dioceses; we were playing around with a primitive version of the Seven Intentions. Even bishops, a kind of CEO position after all, get so bogged down in numbers and financial crises that they can take their eye off their pastoral duties and mission.

I was working closely with the seminary's vice president of administration, responsible for training and educational programs, Melissa Skelton, an ordained Episcopal priest who also happens to have an MBA from the University of Chicago and spent five years working for Procter & Gamble. After three days of workshops, I was exhausted and ready to head to the airport. As I was saying goodbye to Melissa, I raised the subject of my search for a partner. It was a whim. "By the way, I'm looking for a COO," I said. "If you have any ideas, let me know." From her P&G days, she knew a lot of people in the packaged goods business. She had a candidate.

His name was Tom O'Brien. He and Melissa had worked together at P&G. That's how goodness works. I had gone the traditional route, working with headhunters, interviewing candidates; and then, one day when I'm trying to help out some friends, do a little good for free, goodness pays me back. The rest is Tom's of Maine history.

HOW TO BEGIN TO CONNECT

I pray every morning. I get down on my knees in my bedroom and pray. I am not afraid to admit that. Getting on my knees is a way for me to remind myself of my humility in the face of a power outside me, bigger than I. Every morning, I pray for the ability to discern God's will for me that day. This helps me deal with my own disease of self-centeredness, to get out of my own mindset of being in control all the time; praying helps to open me up to God's creation, which includes other people. I cannot change how the world works, but I can change who I am and how I respond to the needs of others.

Sometimes just taking a walk can help. I live within a short walking distance of my office, but occasionally, in the morning, I head out early the long way around through the woods, letting exercise and nature and its sounds distract me from my workaday cares. Others prefer meditation, which I also sometimes use. Too often people use such techniques to distance themselves from the world, to find a kind of silent retreat from the noise and pressure of modern life. I do that, too, but only so that in this silence I can prepare to step back into the human race not as the omniscient boss but as one voice among many.

Volunteering is also a very good way to learn about the importance of connecting. For almost a decade, Tom's of Maine has encouraged all its employees to spend 5 percent of their paid work time volunteering their services to the community. We think this ''5 Percent Solution'' is a great investment in people. I can't tell you how many employees have told me about how their volunteer work has become an important source of joy and fulfillment. Not only does it make them happier around the office, but they often learn skills that help advance their careers. As a result of this volunteer program, my assistant, Joan Matthews, has been teaching adults to read for three years, changing many lives and making a number of friends in the process. In 1997, Joan was named Maine's Tutor of the Year by the Literacy Volunteers of America. Helping other people is immensely satisfying, and once you realize how much good you can do for others, you begin to wonder how much others might be able to help you—if you let them.

MAKING CONNECTIONS

James Newcomb is president of E Source, a company in Boulder, Colorado, that provides information on energy-efficient technology and the energy market to electric and gas utilities as well as corporate energy managers. Begun as a project for the non-profit Rocky Mountain Institute and spun off as a for-profit company in 1992, E Source has experienced a 25 to 30 percent annual growth—earning it a spot on INC. Magazine's list of the five hundred fastest-growing companies in America. A Harvard graduate who worked as an energy consultant for the Carter Administration, Jim says he'd been "thinking a lot about examining one's values within an enterprise or corporate context," which was one reason why he was eager to take part in a pilot program of the Seven Intentions held in Boulder over eight sessions in 1996 and 1997. Jim talked about how the Seven Intentions helped him to connect:

On a personal level I have always identified with the notion that there is something bigger than I am, but, like many people, I didn't acknowledge it in my business life. Let's face it, we're all very competitive. But the opportunity to step back and acknowledge a deeper set of goals and purposes is what drew me to this group in the first place. So I guess you could say that I was looking to connect to something even before I joined the group. There is also a real advantage to doing it first outside your own company in a nonthreatening atmosphere, with people who have expressed a common interest in exploring their values in the workplace . . .

In other groups I've been in, people tended to give the brochure version of their companies. [In the Seven Intentions meetings,] we were very frank about our ups and downs and it humanized the group. Suddenly, you have a perspective of what makes these people. This is definitely something to aspire to in the work world—to bring the whole person to work. Values don't come out of the air; they come from people's experience and their intentions . . .

The process of everyone telling their own stories created a forum to reflect about our own life stories, what we were and what we should be. The group helped us reconnect with our own personal context.

The high point was that it provided one of those moments of intro-
spection, of thinking about the purpose of one's life. There is hardly
any context in day-to-day work in which you feel you can do that. In
a way that's an interesting thing in itself: When our cultures were
more community-based, who people were was more obvious because
everyone knew the family story of who was running the organization.
Now we live in such a transient world, we show up as someone with
a résumé and dive in. The workplace has been more disconnected
than ever. This kind of group helped us reconnect with the personal
context of the people we work with . . .

I found that you could be more open about your sense of a power
outside you, a bigger force with a smaller group of people you know
and with whom you share a common ground. The Boulder group
worked that way. But when I returned to my company to look at its
mission amidst the strains of growth, that piece is not as explicit, at
least not for me as a leader. For many organizations, the leadership
role is allowing other people to come forward. If I blast back and say
I've been to the mountaintop, here's the vision, people tend to pull
back. So some leaders have to be gentler; they have to work to create
the right structures and context to introduce values into day-to-day
business practices. It's a subtle thing. We have big clients like AT&T,
McDonald's. We don't charge in and say we're going to save the
earth (even though many of the people in my company believe they
are in the business of saving the world). We say, "We can reduce
your energy costs by helping you understand new technologies and
finding out more about market risks." We meet our customers on
their own ground, but we are carrying our values with us.

Back at my own company, we have talked about practical measures
for how people run meetings, how to change decision-making. The
most useful aspect of learning to connect is to try to be more open
about values, to have venues to debate them to see if we're on the
right track. . . . Connecting has also cast into light the implicit values
I've used in business, and one of those is that the financial survival
of this business is preeminent—like in any small business. I took this
company on to help endow the nonprofit parent. We took on a significant debt, started out deeply in the hole, and then the market we
thought we were going to sell to—electric utilities—crashed and
burned during the first two years of the business. Our business plan

> was useless. We scrambled like hell to figure out what to do. That's the reality of any small company: How can I make the next payroll and pay the rent? At that point, you have to think seriously about your values. You do have to take risks in the interest of your values.

INTENTION #1 TALKING POINTS

Recognize that there is a force outside of you that is bigger than you. This force is goodness, regenerated by the open and willing attitudes of other people. Join the force.

To embrace the power of goodness, push self-interest and pride aside and align yourself to others.

"One alone is nothing," says Jonathan Edwards. "Being is relation." We are inherently interconnected with others.

Morality is a social relationship that requires shedding egoism.

You cannot be a good business leader without humility and respect for others.

What is goodness?

- Goodness is something bigger than we are—a universal force in the world.
- Goodness is a relation of being to others, according to Edwards. The greater the relation, the greater the goodness.
- Goodness is part of this world, all around us, a kind of spiritual energy that brushes you like the wind.

Discovering goodness is what a spiritual experience is—what Buddhists call "the Buddha nature within us" and Plato called "the higher part of our soul."

To connect to goodness, you must become part of—not the center of—the universe.

INTENTION #1 HOMEWORK

Take some time and be prepared to write down your thoughts on what follows. Better still, begin keeping a Seven Intentions journal. It's important to think about what you've written, hard and honestly. This is a new way of leadership, and to succeed, you must be intentional. It will also be useful to share the results of each homework assignment with a colleague, friend, or spouse. Answering these questions is not a test or competition. It is simply another way to get you to your goal of being a values-centered leader. And remember: To connect, you have to put your ego aside and open yourself to goodness.

Think of an event in your personal life when you found it difficult to connect to another person (e.g., your spouse, a child, a friend, or a parent).

- Why do you suppose you were unable to connect to this person?
- What might you have done differently?

List examples of how your own ego and pride have interfered with your personal relationships.

What kind of spiritual experiences have you had? Write them down and reflect on how they happened and how they affected your life and relationships to others.

Now consider your professional life, and reflect on how you connect to your co-workers.

Does this connection allow others to feel more at ease with you? If so, how?

How do your co-workers connect with you?

What do you think they would say if they were asked the same question about you?

List examples of how ego and pride have affected your relationships with co-workers.

Have you ever experienced a sense of spiritual connection in your work? Under what circumstances?

Discuss your answers to all of the above with a colleague, friend, or spouse.

4

Know Thyself,
Be Thyself

INTENTION #2
Explore who you are, your gifts, and what you care most about in life; these are the clues to finding meaning in your work.

After the publication of my first book, I was giving up to fifty speeches a year. It didn't take me long to note the common denominator among my audiences: They were filled with people who derived no meaning from their work. Many were successful; some were running big businesses or had created their own. Yet they felt something was missing. I suspect you know the feeling. I certainly do. We all know that to be fully human, to grow as a person, indeed, to be happy, is to have meaningful work. One way to achieve such meaning is to include in your work the things you care most about in life.

How do you learn what you really care about, your values? "Know thyself." These were the words carved on the most sacred site in classical Greece, the Temple of Apollo at Delphi, housing the legendary Oracle of Delphi. Five centuries before the birth of Christ, self-knowledge was already viewed as an essential component to becoming a virtuous person. The earliest Greek philosophers had various theories about where such knowledge might come from (divine revelation, science, logic). But true virtue for the classical Greeks, who lived in a class-bound society, was limited to the rich, the well-born, and, curiously, to the beautiful. It was the fifth-century-B.C.E. philosopher Socrates who democratized virtue, arguing, according to his greatest student and biographer, Plato, the revolutionary view that every man, no matter whether he was rich, poor, a slave, or physically ugly, like Socrates, could attain virtue, if he acquired knowledge. For Socrates, the prerequisite of such moral knowledge was self-improvement, what he called "care for your soul." Right action was impossible without right thinking, or, as Socrates most famously put it, "The unexamined life is not worth living." The greatest Jewish and Christian thinkers of later centuries were indebted to this Greek notion of morality. To this day, self-knowledge remains the touchstone of what it means to be a moral person.

Self-knowledge is also the path to meaning. No matter what face we show to our neighbors, bosses, or employees, we are our values. Being forced to go against what we most deeply believe in or care about is bound to cause frustration and misery. No true democrat wants to live under a tyrant. Any person who values respect for others will not enjoy exploiting his neighbors or employees. If you care about the future of the environment, if your passion is standing hip-deep in a sparkling stream, casting for an elusive trout, then you will not find happiness working for a polluter.

As essential as self-knowledge might be, it is amazing how many of us stride through life without admitting our deepest values and passions to ourselves, never mind to others. We are all bundles of secret dreams, desires, and talents. How many times have you been amazed to find out that a friend or colleague (or even close family member) is a passionate collector, musician, car mechanic, gardener, cook, animal lover, you name it? We all care about something, many things, in fact; trouble is, too few of us have been able to, or allowed to, integrate those deep interests into our work life. The result is misery. "There are three things that are extremely hard," wrote Benjamin Franklin, America's first home-grown genius and our first self-help writer, "steel, a diamond, and to know yourself."

How do we come to know ourselves? Self-knowledge does not come in some kind of lightning-like moment of revelation. It is not about being knocked off your horse, like Saul on his way to Damascus, suddenly seeing what your role in this life must be. Coming to know yourself is, as Socrates was the first to explain, a neverending process, a lifelong journey, and an accumulation of moments, teachings, and decisions. That is where your values come from, and the scars often count more than the triumphs.

MY JOURNEY TOWARD MEANING

When I entered divinity school, I thought I was on the lam from the business world, distracting myself with my studies in theology and ethics. I had no idea that my stint as a part-time CEO–divinity student was an opportunity to find out who I was—a businessman who cared as much about his social and environmental responsibilities as he did about making money. My next step was to figure out how I might be able to reconcile my sense of social responsibility with my fiduciary responsibilities as CEO of Tom's of Maine. The breakthrough came in 1989, when I convened that weekend retreat with my board of directors to work out what our company mission ought to be. We identified four key values for the company: (1) customer needs, (2) social responsibility, (3) respect for the environment, and (4) financial success. Yes, we were in the toothpaste business, and wanted to make money at it. But not even the most bottom-line-conscious member of the board was willing to argue that we should be exploiting our workers or polluting the air or rivers of our community to boost profits.

The success that followed confirmed that my intuitions about doing business according to my own values were on the right track. But where did these intuitions come from? How did I, a CEO of what was then a $6 million business, get it into my head that I could create a new kind of American corporation? Conventional wisdom and all the wise advisors I depended on, not to mention the young packaged-goods wizards I had hired, told me that my values belonged in church, not in the marketplace. Business was about profit and loss; it was "amoral." I disagreed, first without knowing really why, which is why I retreated to divinity school. But a decade (and lots of reading and thinking) later, I now know that even back then, in my confusion about whether I wanted to stay in business at all, I sensed that there was an alternative way of running a successful company, a values-oriented way, because of the person I was.

I was my father's son.

HOW I LEARNED THE FACTS OF BUSINESS

I had a storybook childhood. In fact, the pictures in the books I read as a child hardly measured up to the world I was growing up in—thirty-five acres of farm, forest, field, and stream in Massachusetts's Blackstone Valley. We had a big modern house filled with beautiful furniture. There was a barn for the animals. I had my own horse. As soon as the school bus dropped me off at the farm, I ran into the fields and the woods, *my* fields and woods. When I think back on my childhood, I think of nature. Even as a little boy, I recognized how beautiful my world was. It was certainly a privileged life, the farm, the big house, cars, and social standing in the church and town. My father was an entrepreneur who had created a textile business. Like all entrepreneurs, he had his share of failures. But by the time I was a teenager, he and his partners were doing well.

As a kid, I spent time around the mill, getting to know the employees, a diverse group of men and women of varying levels of education. The Pell Woolen Company was a relatively small operation, and my father taught me that each person had an important role in the business. The guy with the pack of cigarettes rolled up in the sleeve of his sweaty T-shirt who worked in the finishing department of a textile mill at an hourly union wage was as important to the success of the company as the salaried manager in the starched white shirt and fashionable tie. My father taught me that for a business to be fully productive, every employee's contribution had to be appreciated. Workers would return your respect with hard work, loyalty, and increased productivity, no matter what their religious, social, or educational backgrounds were. My father respected working people for the best of reasons: He himself started out as one. My father had come from a working family and had never been to college. Because of him, I grew up in a world of social diversity and entrepreneurial creativity.

And then one day I learned that the business had failed and that the bank was going to auction off the house, the furniture, and the cars. We would have to start a new life somewhere, somehow. I was eighteen, a college freshman, and it was a devastating experience. The material things in my life and the social standing that had been part of my identity had vanished. The shock of it all produced a sick, empty feeling that wouldn't go away. My father was a good man; he was also a good businessman. But he allowed himself to be exploited financially by his partners, and the business went down the tubes, taking my idyllic childhood with it. That family catastrophe gave me a stark lesson in business (only recognized years later, of course): The world of commerce itself was not bad, but it depended upon the moral behavior of the people inside it. If they chose to be exploitative, the system would be corrupted. But they could choose to be good, too.

I now know that the teenager who was stunned by how quickly a life of comfort could vanish at the hands of unscrupulous businessmen was bound to turn into the kind of businessman who might want to do business differently. Once you have an emotional experience of this scale and intensity, you develop an inner sense of vulnerability. But that can be a good thing. In fact, I've found it has made me a more perceptive risk-taker. For once you've been to the bottom, you are bound to want to become wise enough to avoid ending up in such a dark place again.

It's who I am.

KNOW YOURSELF—AND YOUR GIFTS

You are more than your genetic legacy and the sum of your experiences at home, school, and church. You are also an aggregate of your talents, the things that you are good at and always were, your gifts. St. Paul, in his First Epistle to the Corinthians, reminds his audience that God works through "varieties of gifts . . . and ministries." He compares such gifts to the body, which is "not one member but many" working in union and harmony. "If the whole body were an eye, where would be the hearing? If the whole body were hearing, where would be the smelling?" Similarly, we cannot all be apostles or prophets or teachers or miracle workers, says Paul. Each of us has to work with his or her special gift.

Over the years, I have learned that my primary gift may be my ability to take a lot of information, much of it seemingly disparate and chaotic, and then synthesize it and shape it into a vision of how things ought to be. It's like being able to see through the fog to the mountain range and then realize that there's a valley beyond those mountains. The early-nineteenth-century British poet and critic Samuel Taylor Coleridge called this kind of shaping imagination "esemplastic." When I started out in business in the late 1960s and early 1970s, you were either on the side of the environment or the side of business. I set out to be both an environmentalist *and* a businessman. My first product was an environmentally safe detergent. Of course, I didn't know it at the time, but in envisioning myself as this strange new kind of businessman who would eventually be selling not just environmentally safe products but values themselves, I was exercising a kind of esemplasticism that Coleridge called "moral imagination."

But as every entrepreneur knows, a good idea is never enough. You have to convince others that your idea is so good that they will not only pat you on the back for being a clever person but also put up some hard cash to help you make your dreams come true. Luckily, my other gift is the ability to promote my ideas to others successfully. In fact, I have always believed that my best talent is my ability to sell. This combination of gifts—to imagine an idea, shape it, promote it, and sell it—is what helps me to keep reinventing my company by refreshing it periodically with new ideas, new products, and new directions (not to mention fresh cash).

That is also who I am, the person with those personal experiences and those God-given talents who has created a successful company and business career. Of course, a lot of things came together, including riding the *Zeitgeist*. Kate and I will admit to a certain lucky timing that our interest in natural products for our own family coincided with the growth of health food stores in the 1970s, which was followed by a burgeoning concern among Americans of all political stripes about the importance of protecting nature. But we worked hard, coped with failure, and turned small successes into bigger ones. Success has a way of blinding you to your defects, and as I mentioned in the previous chapter, my own pride swelled to dangerous proportions. While my talents helped my company grow, my defects kept it from growing faster. It takes a lifetime to figure out what your gifts (and your deficiencies) are. Acknowledging your talents is easy. Copping to your defects takes real self-knowledge and no small measure of courage.

I had to admit to my own powerlessness before I could concede that I was not a perfect husband, father, and CEO. Once I conceded how ineffective I was in all those realms, I became far more effective than ever before. Reaching out for help, I was able to help others more easily. Conceding that I did not know everything about my business, I collected a board of advisors that money could not buy. Recognizing that I was better at inventing a company and products than managing them, I have found a partner who manages brilliantly while sharing my commitment to social responsibility. Freed of some of the day-to-day administrative grind, I am helping to churn out new product ideas, indeed a whole new business; I am also setting up an educational foundation and writing a second book. I am far more effective today than ever *because of what I gave up.*

It is all part of getting to know yourself.

ANOTHER MALCONTENT'S STORY

In Chapters 2 and 3, I told you about my search for a partner to help me lead Tom's of Maine and how I found the COO few people thought existed, Tom O'Brien. After graduating from college, Tom went to work at Procter & Gamble for almost five years, when he began to feel unsatisfied with his career. He thought that returning to school might help him find what was missing. After two years at Harvard Business School, he was thinking about careers in consulting and investment banking. He was even considering starting his own company and wrote a couple of business plans. Procter & Gamble asked him to return to Cincinnati; he resisted, but his former mentors were persuasive and lured him back. He loved it. And for P&G, the feeling seemed mutual. Over the next four years, Tom was rewarded with more and more responsibility. By 1997, he was director of worldwide strategic planning for men's deodorant, an $850 million business. Then the dissatisfaction that had sent him to business school returned. His work no longer seemed meaningful; he began to think that "there must be something else out there." How Tom O'Brien figured out how to get meaning back into his work is a classic example of the Second Intention at work. But let him tell his own story:

> I was working hard and traveling all over the world, having a wonderful time. But then the travel and work began to get to me. Before long, sitting on those airplanes and in those hotel rooms late at night after an exhausting day, I began to realize that I had no time to do the other things I cared about in life besides work. I started thinking about what I liked about my work and what I didn't. Procter & Gam-

ble does a very good job of hiring people they see as individuals who can take initiative, offer leadership, and stand up for what they believe in. I liked that.

I also liked the fact that the company does a pretty good job of operating in a way that is responsible to the communities they do business in. But I wasn't as much a fan about some of the company's approaches to investing. Procter is also a huge place, and the culture can overwhelm you. You either accept their way of life, become "Procterized," if you will, or you start to stick out like a sore thumb. I was concerned that I was turning into a sore thumb. They certainly weren't going to change things because of me. As I tried to assuage my doubts by focusing on what I liked about the company, particularly its integrity, I found myself imagining what it would be like to work for a company that put its responsibility to the community at the center of its business.

As I thought about that more, I suddenly realized that I knew a company that already did that—my own family's business back in Hull, Massachusetts! Our family restaurant and food business is the largest employer in town. When I was growing up, every single Thanksgiving and Christmas, we closed the business down for an open house for the elderly and poor in the community who couldn't afford a holiday dinner. Friends of my parents and my siblings (I'm one of seven kids) would volunteer their help, and we would have this great Thanksgiving dinner. My family still does it. The biggest lesson I learned from my parents is that no matter how tough a situation you might find yourself in, there is always somebody else in a tougher situation, and you should never—no matter how successful you become—lose your compassion for that person. That was at the center of my family's unwritten mission in life and business: Do your part and take care of somebody less fortunate than you. I grew up seeing that, doing it, and realizing what an impact it had on the community I lived in. This kind of generosity was certainly not something my parents had read in a book or heard in a management class. For them, this kind of social responsibility was a given, a non-negotiable obligation you have to your community while you spend time on this earth.

My family did business, but they also did some good. I wanted to do that, too. I finally realized that this was the urge tugging me out

Procter's door. I also knew that the only way I was going to find this kind of social responsibility at the center of the company I worked for was to find my own business. (My father and siblings certainly didn't need my help.) I began thinking of creating a company that was an extension of my own beliefs, my own sense of social responsibility, my own mission to have an impact on the place where I did business and lived, directly and indirectly.

I looked at 233 companies and actually bid on buying six of them. In fact, I was in New York in 1996, having just finished a three-hour meeting with a company I had bid on, when I got in touch with Melissa Skelton, an old friend and colleague from Procter, who was working at General Theological Seminary. I was feeling really good about things. I also wanted to see if there was any way I could convince her to join me in my new adventure. Melissa and I shared a similar vision about how a company can contribute to the lives of its employees and community. We had often talked about how we would run things if one of us were calling the shots. She was interested and told me to let her know when the deal went through.

The deal fell through. Upon careful examination, the company was not all it was cracked up to be. But then Melissa called and asked me if I'd be willing to meet with Tom Chappell. Out of courtesy to her, I agreed. I was familiar with the company from my years in sales at Procter. She mentioned that he had written a book, *The Soul of a Business*. After reading the book, I was less enthusiastic about talking to him. In the book, Tom is very critical about business school people, how they ''don't get it,'' and I'm thinking, ''The hell with this . . . If that's what he thinks, then he shouldn't even want to talk to a Harvard Business School guy.'' When we talked on the phone, I immediately challenged him on his antibusiness school comments, told him he had overgeneralized, that I had spent two years at Harvard Business School (and he hadn't), and that I could assure him that there are a ton of very good business school people out there running nonprofits, not to mention giving a lot of their income to things they believe in. Tom simply said that his experience with business school graduates had not been a positive one. But the reason he was interested in me had more to do with my family business background rather than my MBA. We talked a lot over the next eight months.

I discovered that Tom was looking for someone with a business background to help him transform Tom's of Maine from an entrepreneur's company into an entrepreneurial company with more participation from all the employees. I saw a possible conflict here, and raised it immediately. While he might want to open up the company more to his managers, turn it into a broader partnership between him and his employees, I asked, "Do you really understand what this means, because most entrepreneurs simply cannot make that transition?" I knew firsthand because I had been through it with my own father. When my siblings and I urged him to grow the business, my father's response was, "If I can't count the cash at the end of the night, then the business is too big because I don't want anyone else to do it." Whenever one of us would propose a new idea or suggest a change, he would remind us, "It's my way or the highway."

I pressed Tom on his ability to collaborate and discussed it with members of his board, and finally what I heard from Tom was: "You're right. I like control. And maybe you're going to push me farther than I want to go." He conceded that he was not sure he was capable of making such a partnership work. But he did know that he had worked hard to build the company for several years, and growth would not continue unless he was capable of making the necessary transition. "I want this institution to go on after I'm no longer here," he said. That did it for me. I found my comfort in his honesty, his humility, his ability to say, "I don't know." After months of talking, I finally met Tom and Kate and their family. I visited the company and talked to employees, and I decided to see if Tom's of Maine and what it stood for was for real. It was not so much Tom Chappell that attracted me, not his book, not his board, nor the people working for him. What drew me to Tom's of Maine were its mission and beliefs statements, what the company stood for, and Tom's honesty. I felt that I could truly help the company make the transition from one where the founder had told everybody that they had to operate according to a certain mission to a company that realized they could create more consumer value, greater consumer satisfaction, and better serve the community by operating from a values orientation and making strategic decisions using the mission. I was not interested in "balance." If you talk about a beliefs-centered organization, centeredness is not about balance. The beliefs, these values, have to permeate the organization. They can't come from the top, they can't be grafted on;

they have to be part of what the company is and what it does. Here was my chance to see if I could help them put their values—serving customers, employees, the community, and the environment—at the center of their enterprise.

''Know thyself, be thyself.'' Tom O'Brien was not satisfied with his job. It was not delivering for him, so he thought about it, and then he thought about himself, who he was and where he came from, and, above all, what he valued most in life—and work. And then he made a big change. I think it's a great story—and a perfect example of what I'm getting at in this chapter. You're probably reading this book because, like Tom, you've found something missing. It happens at every level of the game. I was a CEO of my own company, which was growing faster than I had ever imagined, and I was still not satisfied with my career. Tom was running an $850 million division of one of the world's largest companies, and he knew something was still missing. What is that missing element? That's what you have to find out. If you believe that you'd prefer to be managing by values, then you must find out what your values are.

How do you do that? How do you learn who you are and discover what you care most about?

THE I JUST DON'T KNOW CLUB

Over the years, several young people in the community had sought me out for advice about their careers. They tended to be in their thirties, at various stages in their careers, and eager to find work that was fulfilling; but they didn't have a clue as to how to proceed. I didn't have time to advise each person, but I decided that I might be able to help all of them as a group. Their need to find themselves coincided with a new stage in my own efforts toward self-knowledge. The more I listened to the audiences I had been speaking to since the publication of my book, as I grappled with some of the failures of the mission to take hold at Tom's of Maine, and as I contemplated the results of a few crises in my own personal life, I realized I had more to pass on to others than just the message that good values ought to have a place in the business world. What people interested in values-driven business really needed was help in figuring out what their values were and how to integrate them into their work or companies.

I was already trying to come up with a method to train my own executives in values-centered leadership, to make the Tom's of Maine mission an integral part of their own value system and not something that the boss had imposed on them like a company uniform. To this end, I had already begun noodling around with my own variation of a twelve-step program. It occurred to me that maybe by working with these young people, I could get closer to a kind of guidebook, if you will, for this new way of doing business. Tom's of Maine encourages all its employees to spend 5 percent of their paid work time volunteering in the community. In 1995, I decided that my next volunteer project would be this group of young people confused about what to do with their lives, which we eventually nicknamed the "I Just Don't Know Club." Meeting for an early breakfast session of ninety minutes once every two weeks for next six months, we set out to learn about ourselves.

"What are the things that are very important in your life?" was the first question I posed to them. Everyone had a story—about their love of nature, teaching others, helping people express themselves creatively or organize themselves to be more effective. I asked them to read that bit of the New Testament's First Epistle to the Corinthians where St. Paul talks about "varieties of gifts." Then I gave them their first homework assignment: "Think about the one thing that comes most easily to you, what you might call your gift."

This assignment turned out to be more difficult than anyone anticipated, partly because many people find it difficult to discuss what they think they're really good at in public without feeling as if they're bragging. As a result, we tend to hide our gifts even from our closest friends. Discussing this further, we realized that some people hide their gifts even from themselves because it might require a commitment to something beyond themselves, bigger than themselves, which is the source of that gift. That is, after all, the difference between a gift and a skill. While I can learn the skill of how to write a business letter, being able to write poetry is more likely a gift. While practice might improve your poetry, it might never make you a poet. Musical or artistic talent or the ability to solve mathematical problems with ease are gifts over which we have no control; we didn't earn the right to be good at the violin or poetry or algebraic geometry (which is why we are inclined to call such abilities "God-given" gifts).

I encouraged each person in the group to talk about his or her gifts, to tell a story about when their mother taught them to cook, how they realized they were interested in that subject, how one thing or another became what they were so good at. This exploration became a group effort in identifying each other's special gifts, which thus made it easier for people to reveal what they once viewed as a secret. That was the first breakthrough in the I Don't Know Club: to be honest about what you're good at, without embarrassment. The next step was to envision how to use one's gift in service to others, how a certain gift might help make work worthwhile. I asked them to draw pictures of that vision, which they had to show to the others and discuss. In the meantime, they all had been writing about their gifts in their journals. Members came back with such notions as "I think I could be a good teacher . . . or help connect people to nature . . . or help others be more creative." As they envisioned themselves helping other people, they also watched their egos clash with their goals. On the one hand, they were eager for the world to recognize their gifts, while on the other hand, they realized the effectiveness of helping someone with those gifts quietly and without fanfare.

People began describing "jobs" that I had never heard before (e.g., bringing executives into the wild to experience the food they eat and the water they drink; helping business people to be more expressive or creative). "Okay," I said. "Let's turn this into a business." I asked them to think about how they might transform their gifts into a line of work, and to make sure this was more than fantasizing, they would have to write a business plan. The results were remarkable, and three years later, every member of the group is roaring forward in a new career. Through self-knowledge, they were able to envision themselves in a new future. And there is nothing like mutual understanding and encouragement to turn your life around (see box below).

The I Just Don't Know Club also had a big influence on my own future. Working with those young businesspeople convinced me that I could design a practical program to train business executives in values-centered leadership. The following year I worked with a group of CEOs and executives in Boulder, discussing their frustrations in trying to integrate values into their companies and partnerships. Those meetings eventually turned into a pilot program for the Seven Intentions, which I repeated in Kennebunk the following year; both also became a dry run for this book as well as inspiration for a new foundation I have just created—The Saltwater Institute—that will organize seminars in the Seven Intentions and other aspects of values-centered leadership around the country.

As I said, "know thyself" is a lifelong journey. But only when you have a sense of who you are and what you care about can you figure out which directions you want to go in your journey. In the next chapter, I will show you how our values have a way of pointing us in the right direction to what I like to call our destiny. That brings us to Intention #3.

FINDING WHAT WAS MISSING

Like many young people, Dan Erickson had trouble figuring out what he should be doing in life. When we met through mutual friends in the community, Dan had been drifting around from job to job for six years and was currently working as a night watchman at a local hotel. "I was beginning to think that the only thing I was fit to do was be a night watchman for the rest of my life," he recalls. Dan, who ma-

jored in history in college, asked me to help him figure out what he should be doing with his life. I invited him to join the I Just Don't Know Club. Let Dan, now thirty-four, tell you what happened:

The first thing Tom did was ask me to write a mission statement for myself—what I wanted to do. He told me to stop trying to fit into someone else's definition of what they needed and create my own position. I still remember how liberating that was, because it allowed me to talk about what *I* wanted to do, instead of trying to figure out what some employer would want to hear from me. I had always had this vague sense of wanting to be a writer, and I started talking about wanting to reach people from the heart, whether it was in writing or presenting information in a form that was not traditionally business-like. I had been thinking about trying to start my own advertising agency, a kind of freelance creative writing operation, really. What I learned from writing my mission statement was that I did not want to be a certain kind of businessperson. I had this epiphany that maybe the reason I wasn't able to fit into a more traditional business setting wasn't a knock on me but just evidence that I really wanted to do it in a different way. Instead of feeling that I would never fit into the business world, I began to think that I could—but in my own way . . .

The most important thing for me was to think about my gifts: honesty, compassion, and humor. I realized that during the six years I was floating around in the business world, I had put those things on the back burner. In my mind, these were not what an employer wanted to hear in a job interview. Same thing with writing. I wasn't sure what kind of writing I wanted to do, but just being able to admit in public that I wanted to write was great. At first, you have this sense that everyone will think you're crazy. But the great thing about this group was that everyone was coming from the same place of wanting to be true to whatever was in us. Tom encouraged us to answer from our hearts, not necessarily our brains, which made it easier to open up . . .

The biggest breakthrough for me was realizing that I could do anything I wanted to do, as long as I was staying true to myself. Before then, I was lost. I had never gotten on the track. In fact, I felt like, "Jeez, the track doesn't even run by my place." I had reached the point where I had essentially thrown up my hands and said that I cannot really make it in the business world. I had reconciled myself to the idea that it takes all kinds to make up this world, and I was going to be the kind of person who just stumbles through life. With the support and encouragement of this group, I started forgetting about the "I gotta get work so I can get rich and get a wife and a house, etc." and began thinking about what I would like to do. I would walk out of those meetings feeling that I was doing real work in pursuit of work . . .

I came up with a business plan, complete with a brochure and a visual about what my business would look like. All of a sudden, it wasn't just about dreaming. My own plan started out along the lines of an ad agency and ended up being what you might call an "expression company"—that is, a place where customers can get help expressing themselves, communicating what they want to say, whether it's as small as making a birthday card for someone or as big as writing ad copy for their store. And I mean really expressing themselves, getting in touch with what they really wanted to say, sort of in the way that we were in Tom's group. Such a company could use professional copywriters, artists, public relations people . . .

I started this freelance copywriting operation, got a few jobs, and then I learned that Tom's of Maine was looking for someone to write the company's annual report. I put together samples of my writing and brought it to the executive in charge of the project, who hired me. Writing the report went well partly because I found it easy to write about a company like Tom's of Maine, about a values-driven company, because I had learned to find my own values in order to jump start my business career and plan my business strategy. I was asked to stay on to help write the replies to customers who had written the company. Soon I was dividing my time between that and going out and selling. It was amazing. If you had told the person who first started in the I Just Don't Know Club that he was going to be meeting with regional managers and strategic partners of Tom's of Maine to explain to them how the company works, present our creative stuff, I would have told you you were crazy. Back then I couldn't even talk to the person at the pharmacy when I was buying Band-Aids. It was really a revelation in trusting yourself.

In the group, with Tom's help, I learned there was a different way of doing business, one that connected to what you yourself cared about, your values, your gifts. With the support of the group, I was able to take the first steps, which helped me build my self-confidence. At first I thought our little group was about how to find a job. But what really happened is that this group changed my life.

INTENTION #2 TALKING POINTS

Discover your values, those things in life you really care about deeply.

Explore your gifts, your talents.

We learn more about ourselves in community with others than sitting alone in self-analysis.

Discuss your values with other people (i.e., friends, mentors); see what they think about them.

Discuss your gifts with those same people, and get their take on those.

Envision your ideal job.

Create a business plan for that job based on your values.

Apply your values to your current job.

INTENTION #2 HOMEWORK

Again, it's time to personalize what you've learned in this chapter. These suggestions will help you identify your values and your gifts.

Write your epitaph. How would you like to be remembered by colleagues, friends, and family?

List as many values as you can think of. Which of these values came to you quickly? Which ones occurred to you later?

List what you think are the top five values in your life.

5

Envision Your Destiny

INTENTION #3
Envision your future with your head and your heart: Your values in today's world call you to serve. How? The answer is your *destiny*, and as soon as you hear it, this destiny makes total sense.

You can have an ingenious idea or a wizard product, but, as you learned in Business 101 (or the school of hard knocks), you don't have a business until you have vision. The same is true in a values-oriented business. Too many values-oriented people think that it's enough to have the right values. But if you want to compete, a vision is essential. Next you will need a plan to turn that vision into a reality. Your values have to drive you somewhere.

Typically, a company sets a goal and then figures out how to reach it, in terms of time, people, and money. As a personal care products company using natural ingredients, Tom's of Maine might increase its sales in the following way: We could find out what percentage of the public in North America, South America, Europe, and Asia is interested in natural products. That is easily quantifiable. So is how many people, how much promotion and advertising, and how much administration it would take to alert those potential customers to Tom's of Maine's natural toothpaste, deodorant, soap, and shampoo. How much would that cost? Next we have to figure out how to get our products to the stores nearest to those customers. How much will that cost? And so on. It's research, pure and simple, painting by the numbers. The figures essentially write the business plan—at least in a bottom-line-oriented company.

In a values-oriented company like Tom's of Maine, business goals are not directed by outside forces; they emerge from deep inside the company. The Upside Down Manager does not even begin a business plan until his vision is in tune with his values. The values-oriented manager must consider not only if a vision is achievable, but also whether it is right for the company. The history of American business is full of companies setting out brilliantly after an inappropriate goal, one that did not fit with what the company was really about. Tom's of Maine could decrease costs by abandoning recyclable packaging; we would reach more customers by not being so pro-environment, and we could definitely boost our bottom line by never giving a cent away to nonprofit groups. But that is not who we are.

The Upside Down approach is to allow your business goals to emerge from who you are as a company, your essence, your reason for being. Instead of letting the market drive your decisions, you must put the marketplace out of your mind for a moment and ask instead, "Who are we, what do we stand for, and how do we serve?" I am not suggesting you ignore the marketplace. The key is to listen to its call and figure out your unique place in it. What do your customers need, and what is it about your company that can fill and satisfy those needs? What is the role that can be served only by your company? What is unique about you as a competitor?

The answer to those questions is what I call a company's *destiny.* Destiny, in my sense, is not being at the end of a puppeteer's strings, waiting for fate to strike and thus letting your business simply happen. My notion of destiny is an active, purposeful, free (as opposed to predestined) planning process—to take who you are, a company with certain values, to where you ought to be, your unique place in the marketplace. Destiny, as opposed to a mission or goals, suggests a connection between the cultural and competitive values of our beliefs, the particular gifts we possess, and our opportunity to become something that will make a difference in the world. We saw in Intention #1 how the values-centered manager gets connected to a force outside himself, what I called goodness. You are not in business just to profit. With Intention #2, you explore yourself to find out what you care about most in life, and then try to make your own special gifts part of your work. Intention #3 will help you discover where your gifts fit in the world at large and how to devise a plan to get to the position where those gifts will begin to serve the needs of your family, community, and business. Destiny certainly has its spiritual dimension. You will have the sense that there is a grand power calling you forth. It is a vision of your unique potential based on who you are and what gifts you have. If the world is a big puzzle, destiny makes you not only a piece of that puzzle but also helps you find out where you belong. You become the missing piece in a grand vision. You finally figure out your reason for being. But destiny also has a rational dimension. It is also about creating a reasonable plan to get where you belong.

In the past few years, Tom's of Maine has identified its own special place in the international marketplace. The result is that we are now on the verge of a huge new business.

TOM'S OF MAINE'S NEW DESTINY

When Kate and I moved to Maine in 1970, we began what we thought was a personal adventure, a young couple eager to raise a family in a beautiful part of America and create a business that would be in tune with our values. We had no idea that those values, coupled with my gifts as an entrepreneur and Kate's as a gardener and artist, would create a pioneer in natural personal care products, never mind an internationally known company. Looking back, however, what then seemed like a series of struggles, catastrophes, and great good luck now looks like a logical, indeed inevitable, journey. The company we started has reached a position in the marketplace that we never could have imagined, but in another sense, the kind of company it has become has been as inevitable as the rising sun.

Once Kate and I decided not to sell the company, we set out to grow it. But in what direction? After years of success, I was eager to probe deeper into our corporate identity to search for clues as to what direction we might expand in. Once again, I posed the question, "Who are we?" And then I posed the same in another, more challenging way: "What is our purpose, our reason for being?"

This was another way of saying, "If Tom's of Maine didn't exist, what would the culture lose?" It seems an arrogant question at first. But then again, someone has to be the best at what they do, and unique achievements in business have a way of inspiring great changes in the way we live and work. What if Thomas Edison had never existed? What would this country be like without Henry Ford? Or Bill Gates? Without these visionaries, and thousands more, the culture would have been different. They literally changed history. At a more modest revolutionary level, Tom's of Maine has defined *natural* personal care. We were the first into the market with a natural toothpaste and a natural deodorant; we marketed the first natural soap and then created the first natural shaving cream. These products did not exist before the Tom's of Maine label.

Our definition of natural also included some biologically active substances from plants in our products. Our deodorants have lichen, a natural substance that has an antibacterial effect, and our nonfluoride toothpaste has propolis and myrrh, natural compounds with rich historical reputations in oral care, particularly their anti-inflammatory effects. In the early 1990s, a notice crossed my desk about a conference at the Rainforest Alliance in New York where pharmacognosists from around the world, various nonprofit groups, and pharmaceutical companies could discuss efforts to protect potentially useful plants from destruction in the rainforests. Concerned about the future of the rainforest but also intrigued about how pharmacognosy—the scientific study of medicinal uses for plants and herbs—might play a bigger role in Tom's of Maine's products, I decided to attend. I emerged from that seminar appreciating more than ever that the solutions to many medical problems might be found in plants. As part of the company's philanthropy efforts, I pledged $100,000 to the Rainforest Alliance for research into expanding knowledge of medicinal plants in the rainforest. At that meeting, I also met a pharmacognosist and made a deal with him to do some consulting for Tom's of Maine, although he was too busy with his own research to spend as much time with us as we would have liked. By then, however, I was aware of the names of the best researchers in the field, who happened to be located in a few university departments of pharmacognosy and natural medicine. I invited the celebrated University of Minnesota pharmacognosist John Staba to consult for us. Kate and I were reading all we could get our hands on about the biological effects of plants and herbs.

This was all in the air as we were deciding what the purpose of Tom's of Maine ought to be. I was also wondering about our gifts. This, too, was no accident. In 1996 I had organized a "Spiritual Gifts Seminar" for our local Episcopal church. The goal was to help people explore their personal gifts so that they might better serve the church. This got me to thinking more about how Tom's of Maine could better serve its customers. The company mission and beliefs statements drafted back in 1989 explained what the company was about—to be profitable while acting in a socially responsible manner. Almost a decade later, I was asking, "So what? If that's your mission, what are you going to do about it?" How could we as a company serve our customers? What was the best and most productive role for Tom's of Maine in the global marketplace at the beginning of a new millennium?

To answer such questions, we as a company looked inward and tried to understand our core essence. We began to realize that on the way to our unique position in the marketplace, we had learned plenty about goodness, social responsibility, natural ingredients, and, more recently, pharmacognosy. Our successes (and failures) had taught us a lot about serving customers committed to a lifestyle in harmony with nature. They care about the same things we care about. We not only identified a large and loyal market, but we had also become the best at serving it. Obviously, we were a company that had created a hugely successful natural toothpaste, as well as other natural products. I soon, however, began to realize that Tom's of Maine was far more than that. To grab 5 percent in selected regions of the toothpaste market from several international conglomerates, we had to become experts in the natural. My scientists and executives understood the power of herbs, minerals, and plants; they also recognized how those natural ingredients could be assembled in various combinations that satisfied the Tom's of Maine customer's personal hygiene needs.

Therein lay our gift: *We knew natural products and how to serve the people who wanted them.* And thus a new opportunity presented itself. Pharmacognosy was at the center of a revolution in natural health care and preventive medicine. New companies marketing natural vitamins, herbal therapies, and natural preventives were springing up all over the place. Eager to take advantage of the new products, consumers looked on their shelves and saw a lot of new names. Whom could they trust?

Why not Tom's of Maine, a company that had already established itself as the brand leader in natural products? Entering the natural medicines field was the farthest thing from my mind when I attended that pharmacognosy conference at the Rainforest Alliance in New York. But as I contemplated that possibility several years later, it didn't seem like such a big step for us to take. In fact, natural medicines and preventives seemed to me our logical next step. Over the past decade, however, we had not made a move without trying to match it up to our mission and beliefs statements. In early 1997, to help us start thinking strategically about the company's future, I drafted a third document to articulate the company's ongoing process of understanding its future in the marketplace and presented it to the board for discussion and revision. I called it Tom's of Maine's "Reason for Being":

The purpose of Tom's of Maine is:

To serve our customers' health needs with imaginative science from plants and minerals;

To inspire all those we serve with a mission of responsibility and goodness;

To empower others by sharing our knowledge, time, talents and profits, and

To help create a better world by exchanging with others our faith, experience, and hope.

If we were going to look into the future, we would have to be clear about what kind of company we were. The essence of Tom's of Maine was its commitment to bringing personal care and wellness to people through the application of plants and minerals. We are also committed to integrating goodness into our business and passing along what we have learned. I had a sense of what shape the company's destiny might be. I now needed the board to help me and my family to come up with a strategic plan, a road map, for how to get there.

STRATEGIC PLANNING

To create a sense of occasion for board meetings, we try to hold them in different locales, preferably places whose great natural beauty provide us all with a retreat from our workaday worlds that is also inspiring. This meeting of the Long Range Planning Committee of the board and my family took place on the grounds of the Parson Capen House, the oldest house in Massachusetts, located in Topsfield about an hour from our corporate headquarters in Kennebunk. Tom O'Brien had joined the company just a few months before, and this would be his first board meeting. A former board member, Pam Plumb, who is now a professional facilitator, helped us try to envision a new future for Tom's of Maine under this new partnership between "Tom C" and "Tom O," as the employees had begun to refer to us. We split up into three groups to discuss various visions on how to build upon the Reason for Being statement, different options of ownership for the company, how to restructure the hierarchy, and how to house our growing manufacturing and staffing needs.

Tom's of Maine had always been a family company supported by internal financing. We now considered some outside sources of funds: institutional investors, additional debts, convertible debt, direct public offering. In the end, however, we decided that while it was necessary to raise some money, the company would remain in control of the Chappell family. One of the planning groups envisioned a new headquarters that would be a physical space more in tune with the company's commitment to the environment. We spread out the graphic drawings of sixty acres of land the company owns in Kennebunk and began to envision not just a new building but a kind of campus for nature that would include a manufacturing plant and office building featuring lots of original artwork. The complex would be surrounded by a kind of communal green with facilities for child and elder care, even dog care. We went so far as to consider establishing a school of pharmacognosy. I myself was eager to create a learning center to study and teach the practice of building value with values called The Saltwater Institute for Corporate Responsibility, Entrepreneurship, and Creativity.

The family and the board vowed to design a new organizational structure for the company that would flatten the hierarchy and encourage the creativity of every employee. The board renewed the company's commitment to reach out to other people and groups who shared our concerns about nature, the community, and wellness. Most important, we discussed the company's gifts—what as a company we were good at. (And where we were particularly weak.)

We had definitely become good at creating natural products and serving a growing market of loyal customers. Tom's of Maine had established a unique dialogue with our customers, through our package inserts and outserts, and more recently our website, www.tomsofmaine.com, which has become another source of information about our products but also about our volunteer work and philanthropic projects. Creating and experimenting with natural products over the years, and now sitting at the feet of a few of the nation's best plant and herbal researchers, has given us a kind of graduate education in the role of plants, herbs, and minerals in personal care.

Suddenly we realized that this combination of understanding nature and how to deliver it to a growing group of consumers committed to natural products was Tom's of Maine's future. Our destiny was staring us right in the face: No company we had seen in the marketplace had as much interest in protecting the environment and formulating natural products as Tom's of Maine. That was what we were best at as a company—to love nature and to learn how it could serve the needs of our customers. Being the leader in natural care products was rewarding; being the company whose destiny combines wellness, service, goodness, and profit represented a huge opportunity. We were poised to expand from a personal care products company to one that focused on personal wellness. All these ideas we wrote down into another document we called "Six Imperatives" to help guide and shape the future of Tom's of Maine (see box on p. 83).

CHAPPELL "FAMILY PLANNING"

The strategic planning that started with the board continued in a family meeting a few months later. Again, the main topic on the table was gifts. Kate and I were eager to find out what the children really wanted to do with their lives and how we as parents could support them. With the help of Pearl Rutledge, a psychologist and board member, we also raised the question of what kind of responsibility the kids felt to the business and how they, as part-owners, would like to help us out. They made it clear that they had their priorities in life based on their individual gifts. My older sons, Chris and Matt, were already working in the company, but both had dreams of careers outside of Tom's of Maine. Sarah and Eliza were still in college, but they, too, had ideas for their own businesses. (Luke was concentrating on high school.)

Nevertheless, the kids all seemed attached to Tom's of Maine. And a common thread moved through their discussions of their relation to the family company: If they had to spend time at Tom's of Maine before they went out and created their own businesses, what they wanted to focus on was not production or marketing or sales; my kids wanted to create products. And they already had some good ideas that fit perfectly with the board's discussions about the importance of pharmacognosy to the future of Tom's of Maine. Eliza, the aspiring fashion designer, was interested in natural skin care, while Sarah, who loves animals, thought a line of natural pet care products was right up our alley. Kate and I were gratified about how strong their values were. Our kids cared about the environment and the community. What surprised us was their commitment to the future of the company. The business was a stronger part of the family than any of us had realized.

Once the decision was made not to sell, the board and the Chappells went into future gear. And that future was centered around a family-owned company, professionally managed with the help of a new COO and partner for me, committed to serving not just its customers' personal care needs, but their overall health and well-being, what we called wellness. The same customers we supplied with natural toothpaste and deodorants, we would now serve when they were sick with a cough or the common cold, when they were facing menopause, or when they wanted to get going in the morning or relax in the evening. We wanted to help them battle illness and prevent it, with natural medicines and therapies. And while other companies were already in this business, we saw plenty of evidence that consumers were cautious and confused. They wanted a brand they could trust, and we believed that Tom's of Maine was the brand they were looking for.

Serving our customers' personal care needs had been our road to success; serving their wellness requirements seemed to be the right next step. In short, it was our destiny. But to move toward that destiny in a real way required research and development.

THE TOM'S OF MAINE NATURAL WELLNESS CENTER

Our company may have begun as an entrepreneur's idea, but the products came to be only through extensive research and hard science. My original scientific collaborator, Blaine Tewksbury, was a chemist, and chemistry was central to our R&D and thus the company's success. But to expand into the area of wellness, we would have to focus our research more around plants and herbs. Kate and I found ourselves poring over scientific journals in the areas of personal hygiene, natural medicine, and pharmacognosy. By the time our strategic planning began in 1996, the University of Minnesota pharmacognosist John Staba was already consulting for us on the antimicrobial properties of plants that we could use in our personal care products. In the first quarter of 1997, Staba invited one of his protégés from the University of Illinois, Cindy Angerhofer, and Steven Foster, the nation's most prominent herbalist, to give presentations at a company symposium about the use of herbs and plants for medicinal purposes. Over the next few months, I decided we not only needed a full-time pharmacognosist on staff, but that that person should head up our scientific development. Staba was not about to leave his academic position and research, but he thought that Cindy Angerhofer might be tempted to switch over to the commercial sector, and he was right (see box on p. 84). By July, Cindy was head of R&D for Tom's of Maine. But even with Cindy aboard, we realized that we would still need outside help. So we got the most sought-after herbal specialist in the industry, Steven Foster, and the nation's most prominent professional in natural medicines, Norman

Farnsworth, Research Professor of Pharmacognosy at the University of Illinois at Chicago's College of Pharmacy, to be outside advisors.

Over the next year, we expanded our research and development facilities tenfold, from 400 square feet to 4,000, and invested $200,000 in a new laboratory. We hired aggressively. And once we switched R&D over to the acorn method, the new product ideas flowed—seventy of them, from natural cough and decongestant remedies to painkillers, antioxidants, and immunity boosters, from natural elixirs that woke you up in the morning, gave you a boost in the late afternoon, and helped calm you down at night, to herbal teas. We took these ideas to our consumers, and they loved them. As I write this, our scientists are turning those ideas into products that we intend to have in the stores by the time you are reading this book.

ACCEPTING YOUR DESTINY

Not so long ago, I had political ambitions. It did not seem such an outlandish dream that I might be able to serve the people of Maine as governor or in the U.S. Senate. But it was a dream. There comes a time when you have to stop sitting around wondering what you're going to be when you grow up. You are grown up, maybe even in advanced middle age, and it's time to accept the fact that while you may be sending a message to the world about your plans for the future, no one is listening. Sometimes facing up to your destiny is to realize that you will have to abandon a dream, and realize that in this time and this place there is something else that you ought to be doing. If I suggest to the wheelers and dealers of Maine that I'm ready to be governor or run for a Senate seat, I can assure you that I will not get the answer I'm looking for. But every day I get requests inviting me to talk about my experience in a values-oriented business.

My destiny, I have discovered, is to bring together the apparently contradictory worlds of values and business; my calling, if you will, is to prove that while the Bible may say you cannot serve God and mammon, you can. You just have to reorient your business, shift to a whole new paradigm of how business might be done in the next millennium. Luckily for me, the time is right. My message would have been an impossible sell in the 1980s culture of corporate greed; in the 1950s, my claim that a company can be committed to protecting the environment and social responsibility would not have filled any lecture halls. But today, millions of Americans share these values, and a surprising number of top executives are eager to integrate them into their own companies.

One requires a different kind of business plan centered on serving your customers rather than just making money off of them. What is commercial success but filling a current need or creating a new one? That is how you serve your customers. In a values-oriented company, this sense of service is taken seriously. At Tom's of Maine we really do see ourselves as a servant to our customers, employees, trading partners, and communities. We are the sum of all these relationships, which are built on trust. I am also eager to make the company a kind of beacon for other managers and businesses that want to learn about managing by values. This is what is unique about us, how we can play a role in the marketplace and society, not just as a company dedicated to creating good, safe, natural products, but as THE company people can look to for all their personal care and wellness needs.

SIX IMPERATIVES

1. Conveying a personal orientation of respect and service to others;
2. to expand Tom's of Maine branded products into new categories employing pharamcognosy for differentiated values;
3. to build a Tom's of Maine Campus for Nature for all our workspace, play, and hosting of visitors;
4. to create a learning center for ongoing dialogue and teaching of the practice of building value with values, called The Saltwater Institute of Corporate Responsibility, Entrepreneurship, and Creativity;

5. to create an alliance of partnerships from people and groups interested in advancing shared values of the natural world, community, and wellness;
6. to create a governance and structure that empowers and enables the potential of all of us.

WHAT IS PHARMACOGNOSY?

Cindy Angerhofer, the new head of R&D at Tom's of Maine, received her Ph.D. in pharmacognosy from the University of Minnesota and then pursued her postdoctoral studies at the University of Illinois at Chicago, recognized in scientific circles as a kind of Mecca for research in pharmacognosy. Her work at UIC eventually turned into an assistant professorship. Cindy was so busy and happy with her academic research that she couldn't imagine going anyplace else. But she says that she has always been interested in nature and natural products. "In retrospect," she says, "I guess that interest very much shaped where I am today."

I call it destiny. Given her scientific expertise in plants and herbs plus her interest in natural products, where else could Cindy wind up but at Tom's of Maine? But let Cindy, who is still a University of Illinois at Chicago adjunct professor of pharmacognosy, give you a sense of the revolution now taking place as her world of research connects with my world of values-oriented commerce:

Most Americans have no idea what pharmacognosy is, even though it is one of the oldest fields of scientific research. The word is Greek for "the knowledge of drugs," and since drugs originally came from the natural world, from the plants and other things that were used as medicinals, what ancient doctors knew about drugs came from the study of plants. Pharmacognosy eventually diversified into botanists who identify plants in the field, chemists who isolate or extract compounds from those plants, and people like me who are more interested in biology who can look at those same plant extracts for their biological activities . . .

When John Staba, who had been one of my teachers at Minnesota and knew about my interest in natural products, called me out of the blue to tell me that Tom's of Maine was eager to hire a pharmacognosist, I told him I was not really interested in changing positions. John suggested that I visit the company and give a seminar anyway; it might lead to some consulting for the company. What could I lose?

I went to Kennebunk, gave the seminar, and immediately the internal struggle began. Maine is a beautiful place, and I felt immediately at home. I went back to visit again and debated whether I could leave behind the research I had begun at the university . . . On the upside, as an academic researcher I had been frustrated by the distance between the initial and most exciting state of research when you find a biological activity of a plant that no one has ever noticed and actually having a safe, useful product that people can buy. When you do that kind of basic, initial research, you do not often see the light at the end of the tunnel. And that was tough. So one of the real attractions of working for a company like Tom's of Maine was being able to take some of the natural compounds whose medicinal or therapeutic qualities had been validated scientifically and actually create products with them that are safe for people to use.

Of course, I would only want to be involved with a company that wanted to use pharmacognosy in the right way. There are a lot of people doing it the wrong way, trying to exploit the natural way without really caring about the quality of their products or educating their customers. The hype out there is incredible. As much as I believe in my heart of hearts that there is a lot of good to be offered in natural products, it is also a fallacy to say that "natural" means good and "natural" means safe. My standard counterargument to that is that many of the most toxic compounds known to man such as Amanita mushroom toxins, castor beans, and hemlock poison come from nature. If you are not going to do it the scientifically right and responsible way, then bad things get onto the market, which ruins all the good others have done to try to establish herbals as an alternative and a complementary form of medicine the way it is in so much of the rest of the world. Complementary therapy—the idea that we can use things that already exist in the natural world to support and maintain our health—is really important to me . . .

Traditionally, Tom's of Maine has been a company based on chemistry. I am not a formulation chemist. I majored in chemistry in college, so I certainly can talk to chemists, but formulation chemistry is not in my background, and I am therefore very much dependent on the people in our lab doing the formulation to help me along. And while toothpaste and shampoos are foreign lands to me (apart from using them in my daily life), Tom's has been using biologically active substances in their product for years, and in some unique ways. We use rosemary extract as a preservative with an antioxidant for our line of moisturizing and deodorant bar soap. Our deodorants have lichen, a natural organism that has an antibacterial effect. Our nonfluoride toothpaste has propolis and myrrh, natural compounds with rich historical reputations in oral care, particularly for their anti-inflammatory effects. For me, this makes the company's move into natural wellness a continuum. Tom's of Maine has already used natural ingredients in the right way, and I felt confident about coming here and helping the company to take this next step in an equally responsible manner . . .

We also have to take Federal Drug Administration regulations into account. Currently, we have been working on trying to combine over-the-counter [OTC] drugs that are derived from natural products with herbals known to have complementary effects, though the FDA has yet to recognize it. For example, right now we have a prototype for an expectorant syrup with guaifenesin, the only FDA-approved expectorant for over-the-counter sale. Guaifenesin comes from guaiacol found in trees and other plants. All the major manufacturers create guaifenesin synthetically by adding a glycerol molecule to synthesize guaiacol. We have not been able to find anyone making guaifenesin from natural guaiacol. We have made the prototype using a synthetic guaifenesin, which, of course, is not acceptable within Tom's of Maine's mission to use natural ingredients. So we are probably going to have to contract someone to prepare guaiacol naturally from a forestry waste product. That will make our syrup more expensive to produce. But the good news is that Maine is a perfect source for forest products. Tom Chappell has conferred with the governor's office about how the company might collaborate with others in the state so that we can source guaiacol naturally and produce a federally approved over-the-counter drug that not only meets the FDA requirements but stays within the company's mission . . .

We are also working on a natural decongestant with the FDA-approved ingredient pseudoephedrine, a starting compound derived from the plant *Ephedra sinica*. We've managed to find a commercial source for pseudoephedrine. The FDA has very strict and well-laid-out guidelines for the concentration of pseudoephedrine allowed in a decongestant. And that causes a dilemma for us: To make a stable product, especially in the cough and cold area, requires a lot of filler. The usual filler is alcohol, which we will not use. That creates a major formulation problem for both the OTC drug as well as the herbals because many of these extracts do contain alcohol, and if you drive them down to where there is no more alcohol and then put them into a water environment, the extracts do not tend to dissolve well; they just sit there. To solve this problem, we have used things with a natural solvent ability, like glycerin. We also do not use dyes or artificial flavors, and we use honey instead of artificial sweeteners.

This is a booming area. The laws are changing constantly. I am confident that Tom's of Maine will make a big impact. There's a lot of education that needs to be done regarding these natural herbal therapies. Customers are confused and looking for someone to trust. There has to be a certain level of integrity that goes along with a product. Customers look at shelves full of different echinacea products, for example. Many of them are simply not labeled correctly. They do not have the Latin name of the plant, which is essential. European countries demand that. If you do not know the species of echinacea you're using, you really don't know what you're getting. That has to be on the label. I also think that you have to be clear about where the species is grown in the world and under what climatological conditions, which definitely affect the active ingredients. That presents a particular dilemma with echinacea because its active compounds are not known. We have an idea, but it is very difficult to standardize them. That is true of many natural remedies, which means even a supremely ethical company like Tom's of Maine is going to have a hard time figuring out how to deliver quality natural products consistently.

Where a plant is grown makes a huge difference. I remember picking up a bunch of pepper plants, jalapēnos, at a farmers' market in Minneapolis. I didn't have room for all of them in my small garden, so I gave half to my brother for his garden in St. Paul, ten miles away, same weather. But we have different soil. He put a lot of humus, manure, and fertilizer around his plants, and I simply watered mine. I could pick mine and eat them like a tomato. They were very good but not particularly hot. Those same peppers grown in my brother's garden, ten miles away, were absolute fire. Where a plant is grown makes a big difference. That is part of the wonder of plants. There is a complexity of interactions in what a plant is made of that we still do not know. In many herbals there are as many things acting antagonistically as synergistically; sometimes there are things that we do not consider the active component, yet it contributes one way or another to the overall effect we get from the plant. So there is a lot of wonder to it yet, which is something that turns off the FDA and other regulatory agencies who want one compound isolated to call that the drug. That's why we're committed to education and more research. We do not want to jump on the hype bandwagon. We would prefer to put things that have been tested carefully and have a long history of efficacy into a product, and then try to inform our customers to the best of our ability what benefits they can expect—and cannot expect. There is not enough of that in the industry right now. We are in the business of helping prevent illness, which is different from having a headache and reaching for a pill that will get rid of it quickly. We need to do a job of explaining to people that when they take echinacea, they probably will not feel instantly better (and if they do, it is unlikely to be the echinacea that did the job). That is not the way these natural remedies work. We need to provide the education to make sure that people do not have expectations beyond what these remedies can do.

Tom's of Maine is committed to educating the public about these products, and with my own background in education this is a great concern to me. We have been talking about having a kind of institute of pharmacognosy here, pulling together experts from the fields of medicine and natural medicine as well as hard science. It is an expensive way to go, but it is the responsible way to go. In fact, it is the only way for Tom's of Maine to go because it is part of the company's "Reason for Being"—to share its knowledge with others.

INTENTION #3 TALKING POINTS

Your main goal is to figure out how you can serve your customers and your community. To commit yourself to this notion of "servanthood," you must know who you are and what you stand for.

To serve best, you should know what is unique about you (or your company).

You must envision what the world would lack without your company's contribution. The result is your vision of your destiny.

It is generally your values and your gifts that will help you generate a vision of how you can make a difference in the world.

Once you discover your destiny, accept it and step into it. (Warning: Accepting your destiny may require abandoning a dream.)

The values-oriented company never exploits its customers, it serves them.

Create a set of imperatives for your enterprise.

And once you have your destiny clearly in mind . . . go for it!

Warning: Fulfilling your destiny requires more than gifts and a vision. Above all, stepping into your destiny requires *courage*.

INTENTION #3 HOMEWORK

Your destiny will flow from what you've learned about yourself in Intention #2. To find out where you're going, you first must know who you are, what you value deeply, and what your special gifts are. Think about the following issues. Again, you'll need someone to bounce your thoughts off of.

What have you been put on this earth to be? To do? To accomplish?

Given your special gifts, envision how you'd best like to use your talents to serve others.

Discuss the results with someone who knows you *and one* you trust. What is this other person's take on your destiny?

If you didn't exist, what would be missing from your culture? (We call this the "It's a Wonderful Life" exercise.) How would your family be different? Your circle of friends? Your neighborhood? Your work?

Write a rough draft of your own personal vision statement.

Think back on those times when your destiny might have been pulling you in its direction, when you were considering doing what you thought you were born to do. What held you back?

Chances are that the biggest obstacle to stepping into your destiny has been (and will be) *fear.* Everyone has felt it. No one is eager to step into the abyss. But to be a values-centered leader, you have to have courage. Think about this, long and hard.

And then write in your journal your strategies for dealing with your fears and other obstacles in order to pursue your destiny.

6

Seek Advice

INTENTION #4
Every leader makes mistakes, which is why the values-centered manager never makes a decision without using the secret weapon of Managing Upside Down—a diverse group of expert advisors.

Congratulations, you're halfway through your training in Managing Upside Down. You've been working on setting your ego aside and connecting to goodness; you've explored yourself and identified your gifts and the things you believe deeply—your values. You have considered what it is about your business that distinguishes it from others in the marketplace, and with your values driving your enterprise, you're ready to move toward your ultimate goal, what I have called your destiny. I suspect you're brimming with a million ideas and strategies for how to make it happen.

But are they the right ideas, the right strategies? Are you certain about that destiny? How do you know that what you're doing is even in the ballpark? If you're like most people I know in positions of power (including myself), you are probably not inclined to admit to something less than omniscience. You prefer giving orders to taking advice. You're supposed to know what you're doing, and to seek the advice of your subordinates might be taken as a sign of weakness. And what sane leader wants to appear weak?

But in the real world, all leaders make mistakes, even values-oriented leaders. So before you can act on the results of Intentions #1, #2, and #3, you have to take advantage of the Upside Down Manager's secret weapon: *seeking the advice of other people.*

The first three Intentions have been all about you: By opening yourself to goodness, you have become part of something bigger than yourself, and by exploring your values, you have a keener sense of your gifts and a vision of how to serve. Intention #4 is about expanding this circle of one into a complex and diverse group of advisors. The Upside Down Manager knows that by seeking advice he or she will not seem weak, but will in fact become more powerful. Knowledge is power, and true knowledge comes from a variety of sources, including failure. After all, values-centered leadership is all about turning the traditional business pyramid upside down and recognizing that wisdom can reside outside the confines of the boss's office.

In fact, wisdom is all over the place—among your co-workers and family members, in your churches and synagogues, on the streets and in your communities. You simply have to train yourself to take advantage of it. I am not talking about group therapy or political organizing. The kind of advice I have in mind is at the level of your soul. You reach out to people you respect, who are willing to listen and share in your destiny and help you achieve it. It is an extraordinary kind of exchange, intellectually and spiritually. Self-interest is kicked aside; brutal honesty and total support reign. Who wants false advice or half-hearted support? No matter how successful you've been, no matter how experienced or how brilliant, you are bound to be more successful, become more experienced, and be exposed to more brilliant ideas than any one woman could generate through the advice of others. You will also end up turning a bigger profit.

This is a lesson that I have had to learn over and over during the past thirty years.

E PLURIBUS UNUM: OUT OF MANY ADVISORS, ONE SUCCESSFUL CEO

Kate and I started our business with a $5,000 loan from a lawyer friend of ours named Dick Spencer who, like us, had moved back to Maine to find a better life for himself and his family and believed that environmental protection and profit could prosper together. In the early years, Kate was preoccupied with the children and Dick was working for Ralph Nader on environmental issues in Maine. That left a lot of the day-to-day imagining and business to me, the son of an entrepreneur and a born salesman, to be sure, but also an English major with almost everything to learn about business. I attended a few seminars for entrepreneurs, but generally I was learning by doing. My best teacher was trial and error. And then I got lucky.

I found Fred Scribner. On second thought, it had nothing to do with luck and a lot to do with goodness. At the time, I was helping the University of Maine's marine research center with a gasoline contamination problem in their artesian wells. Ed Myers, a Maine entrepreneur and businessman who was then assisting the center's director, had asked for my help, and one day while we were working Ed asked me if there was any stock in my company for sale. I could use the cash, but I had no idea how to give stock. I needed some legal advice. I decided to call a Portland attorney I had met at a statewide meeting of the Episcopal church who I was sure would have the answer. Fred Scribner was one of the most experienced and influential corporate lawyers in the state of Maine. Fred remembered me, we arranged a meeting, and he proceeded to set me up to sell stock in a private offering. I then made an appointment for lunch with Ed Myers, who, using the back of a paper placemat, showed me how to establish value and motivate a minority shareholder to buy stock. I asked him if he would buy stock in my company on the basis of that valuation. He signed on. Using Ed Myers's strategy and Fred Scribner's legal counsel, I approached some other people and proceeded to raise a much-needed $125,000 for my fledgling company.

I did not go searching for a financial advisor. Through my church connections and by helping with the university's environmental problem, I got the advice I needed to take my business to the next level. Within a year, I was selling our nonphosphate liquid laundry detergent to health food retailers and met Paul Hawken, president of the natural foods distribution company Erewhon Foods. Paul, a legendary pioneer in the health food business, liked our pollution-free laundry detergent so much that he suggested we develop a line of hair and skin products that he could distribute to natural food stores. With Paul's generous advice and coaching, Kate and I began doing some research on the kind of people who shopped in health food stores and were struck by the values we shared with them. We then hired a chemist, named our company "Tom's Natural Soap," and went to the market with our new Apple Shampoo, Rosemary Crème Rinse, Pure Plant Lotion, and Cocoa Orange Soap.

CREATING AN ADVISORY BOARD FOR A FAMILY-OWNED COMPANY

For the first twenty-five years, the biggest influence on Tom's of Maine was Fred Scribner, a politically conservative Maine attorney who died in 1995 at the age of eighty-seven. Fred, the Platonic ideal of a generous and wise man, counseled Kate and me on business and family matters. We had our political disagreements. (On the matter of whether the Democrats had anything constructive to say, we simply agreed to disagree.)

The best advice he ever gave me was, "Maintain control of your company." He told me that the biggest disappointments he had seen in his lifetime had happened to people who had sold out too soon.

He would tell me story after story of family companies in Maine who sold out and regretted it. The family, he advised, should control a family company. I pushed back many times on this point. When we were trying to grow the company, cash was a major problem; we were on the edge. We considered venture capital, we considered going public, we considered all sorts of things, and all the while, Fred Scribner said to me: "Owning the majority of your company is my counsel to you, period." And here we are, virtually a $30 million company, and the Chappell family owns more than 70 percent. That is extraordinary, and it is mainly due to Fred Scribner, whose words were a great consolation to Kate and me when we decided not to sell the company. Since his death, Fred Scribner's legacy to Tom's of Maine has been so magnified that to me and Kate and the board, he lives on as "Mr. Scribner," truly a founding father of Tom's of Maine.

Realizing how lucky I was to have one of the state's premier legal minds on my side, I set out to find more Fred Scribners. During the first ten years of the company, I understood that I needed to attract people much wiser than I to my side—for free. And then I had one of my best ideas ever: I, a green, thirty-year-old entrepreneur, would approach experienced men and women in their fifties and sixties and ask them if they would be willing to talk to me about business. Scared at first, I soon realized that the worst that could happen was that they would tell me to take a hike. I began by approaching one person at a time. More often than not, they were flattered that this aspiring entrepreneur wanted to sit at their feet, and the information flowed.

In the seventies, we had a small group of investors whom I included in the company's biggest decisions. But in 1980, I made a quantum leap in the business advice and expertise available to me. I met John Rockwell, a partner in the New York consulting firm Booz Allen & Hamilton who had recently bought a house in the Kennebunk area. His wife told him about this young couple who had started a new toothpaste business located in Kennebunk's scenic old train depot. Curious about the kind of entrepreneur who thought he could break into a market dominated by the likes of Colgate and Crest, John dropped by the depot for a chat, we hit it off, and he has become my mentor, advisor, and friend of almost twenty years. What a lucky day! Rock's arrival into my business life was like a Little Leaguer having Ken Griffey giving him batting practice. Rock took an immediate interest in what Kate and I were doing, and we knew we were blessed to have a man sharing decades of experience in consulting for all sorts of companies, small and large, including General Electric, DuPont, and General Foods. Rock's intuitive feel for business is probably his most impressive gift as a business consultant. His specialty at Booz Allen was helping companies create a competitive advantage. He was the one who suggested that we might shift the image of the company from a tiny mom-and-pop operation to a stronger player in the health food market by making the most of what we had in common with the state we lived in: a strong, positive tie to nature. Connecting our pure, natural products to the mystique of Maine was a perfect fit, and thus "Tom's Natural Soap" became "Tom's of Maine" (see box on p. 114).

Soon I was also benefiting from the experience of Pearl Rutledge, a psychologist specializing in organizational development whom I met at an executives' effectiveness conference where she was a facilitator. Not long afterwards, I attended a management seminar at Dartmouth's Tuck School of Business where I met the new dean, Colin Blaydon, who was willing to answer my questions about growing a business. At first I was just a struggling entrepreneur picking the brains of the pros. But then Fred Scribner helped me formalize the idea of a board of directors, an unusual notion for a small private company.

In 1981, I assembled a small group of impressive advisors, including Spencer, Scribner, Rutledge, Blaydon, Rockwell, Anne Osborn, another early investor, and Pam Plumb, the former mayor of Portland, into a formal board that met four times a year, reviewing financials and marketing plans and trying to look ahead. It was to

this group of advisors that I went in 1986 with the news I intended
to spend half my workweek as a theology student at Harvard Divinity
School. And nine months later, when I invited a Harvard Divinity
professor to give them a seminar on the thoughts and beliefs of the
Jewish philosopher Martin Buber, this was the group that did not
send out for the men in the white coats. I eventually added to their
number Ruth Purtillo, an ethicist whom I had met at the divinity
school, where she was teaching a course, and Reverend Philip Allen,
an Episcopal priest who is also a Lakota Sioux.

In 1989, it was the board of Tom's of Maine that spent a weekend
in a beautiful hotel located where the Kennebunk River meets the
Atlantic Ocean hashing out the company's mission and statement of
beliefs. A decade later, I can say without a doubt that producing
those two documents was, in my opinion, the board's most significant contribution to the success of Tom's of Maine.

These were people who knew more about business than I did, and
my management appreciated the fact that I had this kind of counsel.
We eventually increased the number to twelve, adding some investment banking expertise. Today's board includes A. Heaton Robert-
son, who oversees the banking and investment activities of Brown
Brothers and Harriman's Boston office; Paul Duffley, vice president
of trade relations for Pepsi; and Dr. Ray Williams, a world-class
periodontist who was the former assistant dean of the Harvard Dental
School and is now the head of the periodontology department at the
University of North Carolina. In the early 1990s, we were struggling
to get the American Dental Association's approval for our natural
toothpastes. In fact, we were not quite sure how to go about it. Then
I met Dr. Ray Williams, who was not only a prominent academic
figure in dentistry around the world but was well known in the toothpaste industry. He was willing to hear the Tom's of Maine story and
take a close look at our products and what we were trying to do,
and in 1994 he agreed to help us. In less than a year, we got the
ADA seal of approval. If I have an idea that I am not sure about in
the field of toothpaste, I take it to "Dr. Ray."

A small company can increase its knowledge and expertise, not to mention its clout, by bringing in major business figures as advisors. In 1995, I was attending the Chain Drug Industry trade show. We were working hard to increase our presence in such mass-market stores as Walgreen, Wal-Mart, CVS, and Safeway, and I, quite frankly, was feeling like a cork bobbing in their ocean. During dinner, I was introduced to a man at my table who not only seemed to know everyone at the table, but everyone in the hall of about one thousand people. His name was Paul Duffley, a top Pepsi executive, who, I later learned, was beloved within the industry for the good will he had engendered in trade relations beyond his responsibilities to Pepsi. I told him a little bit about Tom's of Maine, and we made an appointment to talk the next day during the trade show, when I unloaded on the poor guy my frustrations about the business and told him I needed an advisor on these major accounts. Would he be interested? He was, to my amazement. We asked Paul Duffley to join the board, and his name opens doors for us all around the country at the CEO and VP level of major companies. Recently we added to the board another financial expert, Dan Pierce, chairman of Scudder Kemper Investments in Boston.

It's an impressive group. Tom's of Maine now has world-class counselors on its board from the fields of dentistry, mass-market trade relations, business consulting, psychology, law, ethics, and investment banking. They are one of the company's greatest assets. Without this diverse and imaginative group, I'm not sure I would have had the courage to reconsider our decision not to sell the company. That we had a Plan B (i.e., to find a COO/partner for Tom Chappell) was because members of the board thought that was a good way to go. When I proposed the possibility of a new business in plant medicinals, this diverse group of advisors was there to bat ideas around. With my family and my board, I was able to envision another future for Tom's of Maine that was far more complex and interesting (and potentially profitable) than just dreaming up another toothpaste flavor.

Family businesses do not typically have that kind of power on the bench. What we do at Tom's of Maine is what I like to call "swamp marketing." You head on your journey never knowing what you'll step on, whether you'll end up on a dry spot or find yourself trudging through the muck. That's the way it is for entrepreneurs. But believe me, you can make the journey a lot drier and safer with a professional group of advisors protecting your back.

As I look back, I realize that our board has helped Kate and me to grow up. We have gone from twenty-seven years old to fifty-five in this company, positioning Tom's of Maine to have a real chance at making an impact on society. That's pretty amazing. And it's not something that I did alone.

In addition to our board, Kate and I discovered another treasure house of good advice—our customers.

LISTEN TO YOUR CUSTOMERS

Early on, the board and I realized that if Tom's of Maine was to become the kind of original company we wanted it to be, one that led the market rather than followed it, we had to cultivate a close relationship with our customers. We did not get our ideas from some outside think tank; we would not follow the willy-nilly trends of the industry. We decided we would create the trends. The success of Tom's of Maine, we reasoned, would be directly related to the needs of consumers. After all, this was why Kate and I had gone into the personal care business in the first place: to create the very kind of natural products that we wanted for our own family that were not available on the market. We had no scientific or demographic information that there was a market for such products beyond the Chappell family. But Kate and I had an intuition, a gut feeling, that we were not alone.

We were right, and we began establishing an unusually strong and personal relationship with those thousands of Americans who shared our values through health food stores. At the end of our first decade, the company's sales stood at $1.5 million annually. Our destiny seemed to be tied to the health food industry. But we stayed in close touch with our customers, inviting them on our packaging to write to us about our products, and they did. By the early 1980s, we began to sense that natural was going mainstream, and that tens of thousands of potential Tom's of Maine customers might not shop in health food stores. To get to them, we'd have to find our way onto the shelves of supermarket and drugstore chains. We discussed this with the board, and in 1981 we decided to shoot for a wider market. Everyone in the health food industry thought we were crazy. Outside consultants looked at us and said, "You are absolutely nuts to take on Procter & Gamble. They will kill you."

Were we crazy? We decided to check with our ultimate source of commercial wisdom—the consumer—and the results went against the conventional wisdom. Twenty-five percent of the adult population of America, we learned, was interested in trying a natural toothpaste, shampoo, or deodorant; but only 2 percent of them wanted to go to a health food store for it. Almost one quarter of America had advised us that they were interested in trying our products, but only if we brought those products to them. And that meant sitting on supermarket and drugstore shelves next to P&G, Colgate-Palmolive, and the other big boys. The board agreed with this strategic expansion, and the company, particularly with the expert guidance of John Rockwell and Colin Blaydon, was able to find a small space on the shelves of supermarket and drug chains. Soon the split in our sales was 20 percent mass market and 80 percent health food stores. I remember Rockwell predicting that within five years those numbers would be reversed. "Not if it is at the expense of our health food customers," Kate warned.

We certainly did not want to antagonize the very people crucial to our success; health food stores had believed in us from the beginning, and I had a personal relationship with virtually all the owners. Our research, however, revealed that 10 percent of our health food retailers would scream "Traitor!" at our move outside the health food industry, and would kick us out of their stores. The board, Kate, and I finally agreed: If we wanted to grow, we would have to risk the hostility of our old friends in the health food market. John Rockwell and others assured us that if we got hold of a 50 percent share of the health food market category, the stores could not throw us out. Their customers—our customers—wouldn't stand for it. We decided to follow the customers. What I did not know at the time was that we were beginning to create a growing circle of advisors for Tom's of Maine of incredible diversity. I had to learn that piece of business in divinity school.

THE "COMPLEX BEAUTY" OF DIVERSITY

In a class about "Miracles and the Gospels" taught by the feminist theologian Elisabeth Shussler-Fiorenza, we were discussing the relationship between Jesus and his disciples during Christ's final days. The author of the Gospel According to Mark seems to be stressing that from the time of Jesus' arrest to his disappearance from the tomb, his most loyal disciples were not the men who followed him but the women. Judas betrayed him, and Peter, "the rock" on which Christ said he would build his church, deserted him. As Jesus languished on the cross, his male followers were nowhere to be seen. But the women were there at the foot of the cross. They also appeared at the tomb.

I remember so clearly sitting in that classroom, listening to this unusual interpretation of the gospel from a woman's point of view, and suddenly realizing, to my horror, that I had not given my wife Kate the credit she deserved. In the Gospel According to Tom, I had seen myself as playing a larger role in making a go of the company than Kate. She had helped me see the world not only from a woman's perspective, but also from the family perspective and the consumer's perspective. As an artist and poet, she also brought a kind of creativity that is rarely found at the top of most companies. Since day one, she had been pivotal in our new-product research and development. While I had to work constantly at employee relations, sensitivity and compassion for her fellow workers was second nature to

Kate. (I can't tell you how many people over the years have confided to me or to the press how Kate managed to salve injured egos after I left the room. "She is the reason Tom has not irreparably shot himself in the foot over all these years," one "informed executive" told *The New York Times.* "She is as good a listener as he is a talker.")

Here I was learning about the importance of a woman's point of view in a graduate school classroom when I had been benefiting in my business from one particular woman's several different points of view for almost twenty years. I vowed to give Kate her due.

Divinity school turned out to be a constant lesson in the value of diversity. Every day, I sat in class with women and men half my age, with Asians, Indians, Europeans, with homosexuals. I spent days and nights discussing philosophical and theological issues or just life and work in general with all sorts of people who were different from me. (It didn't take me long to realize that the real weirdo in that multicultural class of divinity students was the gray-haired CEO of the toothpaste company in Maine.)

It was a beautiful thing.

In another class, about Jonathan Edwards, the eighteenth-century New England theologian who became a major inspiration for my new way of looking at business, I learned why. For most people, beauty means a kind of balance or symmetry. You look at an object or a painting or a room, you hear a poem or a piece of music, and it gives you this good feeling, a tingling in your spine or goose bumps; it strikes you as beautiful. If asked to explain what is beautiful about those things, we are inclined to say that it holds together, it has its own integrity, or, in the simplest terms, it just works. Edwards calls this "simple beauty."

Edwards offers a second kind of beauty, a beautiful thing that at first sight might not seem beautiful at all. But when you look at it more closely, when you contemplate it, look deeper into it, explore it, you notice things you had never seen before, subtleties, complexities, maybe even a kind of profundity. And then you realize that this, too, is beautiful. Edwards calls this "complex beauty." I remember a wonderful experience years ago that proved this very point in a simple though startling way.

Phil Allen, our board member who is both an Episcopal priest and a Lakota Sioux, met with the entire company, which in those days numbered about fifty. It was a pretty typical group of Maine people who had worked together, some of them for years. If you had asked any of them whether we knew each other well, we would have said yes. We were colleagues and friends. With this group sitting before him, he simply asked all the men to stand. They did, and it was a large group. He then asked the women to stand, and they did. He asked only the fathers in the group to stand, and then the mothers. No big deal. Then Phil asked the single mothers to stand. That was interesting. He asked the single fathers to stand. That was really interesting. Suddenly we were learning things about our fellow workers we did not know. He asked those who wanted to have a child to stand up, and several people did. That was a revelation! And then he asked an amazing question: "Would all those who have *lost* a child please stand up?" A few people stood up, and a few more joined them. Others in the audience were stunned. We had no idea. You wanted to start crying right there and then! He also asked those with a Hispanic background to stand. He went through other ethnic groups as well.

Phil Allen's simple questions took the audience through various layers of the lives of people in that room. Suddenly we were finding out amazing things, private things, perhaps once-secret things, certainly things about people in our community that most of us did not know. We began seeing people we thought we knew well in an entirely different and deeper way. "Look how different you are," he pointed out, "even though you have something in common, working at the same company." At the end of the meeting, Phil led us into an open field and asked us to hold hands, form a circle, and look around at everyone and affirm this entire circle of Tom's of Maine employees. Immediately we had a sense of solidarity among all the differences we had just learned about. Then he asked us to turn around and face outwards, still holding hands. "You will have to face the world, but now you have the strength to implement the company's mission because of the solidarity gained from all those differences bound together in a common cause."

We had experienced complex beauty. It was an extraordinary and extremely intense moment. "Particular disproportions greatly add to general beauty," Edwards wrote in his essay "The Mind." The more complex the beauty, according to Edwards, the more apparent its dissimilarities, the more intense that beauty can become.

DIVERSITY IS NOT ONLY BEAUTIFUL, IT'S GOOD BUSINESS

I began to see my customers and employees through Edwards's eyes. Different ethnic groups, different skin colors, different accents, different levels of education, different backgrounds, which might seem chaotic close up. But I realized that if my company was going to succeed at selling our products to a mass market, we had to know our customers better, we had to see the world from their perspectives, and that meant enlarging the variety of points of view around the office.

My managers and I had been inclined to hire in our own image. You want to be comfortable with your co-workers, and you are likely to think that what's familiar will be more comfortable. Yet comfort and sameness are not usually the best ingredients for creativity; different points of view, a variety of opinions, some tension, not to mention intensity, stir up the pot, and the result can be very creative. Women do see the world differently from men, and so do Native Americans, blacks, and Asians, not to mention religious people and those who are educated and not so educated. It is amazing to me, in retrospect, that I and my fellow business leaders spent decades keeping women out of executive positions in areas such as marketing in spite of the evidence all around us that in our culture women were traditionally more responsible for the shopping than men and are thus more experienced consumers. By understanding the value of those different perspectives, we can begin to see a new kind of harmony in the world, a new beauty, but in a more complex world.

Now, when I look around the room at one of our own staff meetings, I am amazed by our progress at getting different perspectives into the circle: I'm a WASP entrepreneur with an MA in theology; Kate is an artist, poet, and marvelous cook who helped found and grow a $30 million company while she raised five children (just writing that leaves me in awe); Tom O'Brien is from a large, Irish Catholic family in Massachusetts in the fish and restaurant business who graduated from Harvard Business School and ran an $850 million division of one of the biggest (and most successful) companies on the planet before he became my COO; Melissa Skelton, my head of brands, is an ordained Episcopal minister who also has an MBA and worked for Procter & Gamble. A quiet middle-aged guy in sales had worked for the company for years before anyone found out his previous career: He had been a policeman and had actually written a novel about his experiences on the streets.

Some heads of personnel might look at a cop-salesman or an MBA-female priest askance. How could such a person fit in? But in the Upside Down company, such an odd assortment of credentials is a perfect fit. We are about to hire eight new people for leadership roles in regional business, brand, and product development. I told our recruiters that I wanted diversity, ethnic as well as gender. Over the past decade, we've done quite well in wiping out the men's club atmosphere that used to exist in our corporate offices. Our managerial ranks are now 50 percent women! Of course, women have been sitting on our board of directors since its creation and now make up one third of the board. Ethnic diversity has been a lot more difficult for the company, mainly because of our location (the population of Maine is less than 2% black and Hispanic). But these new positions will be outside of Maine in metropolitan markets around the country, and we're hoping to recruit executives from those areas who will begin to help us make our management as diverse as our customer base.

A NEW BUSINESS, SOME NEW ADVISORS

Once I was alerted to the prospects of natural medicine, I was eager to learn more. Kate and I began reading widely about herbal and plant remedies and therapies. I even hired one plant expert I met at that Rainforest Alliance seminar I attended to consult, but he was too busy with his own research to give me the time I needed. By then, however, I was aware of the names of the best researchers in the field, who happened to be located in a few centers of pharmacognosy and university departments of natural medicine. I turned to my tried-and-true method of getting on the phone and introducing myself to these experts, assuring them how intent I was to put pharmacognosy at the center of my new product development. That networking soon led me to John Staba at the University of Minnesota, who signed on as a consultant. When I told John I wanted a full-time pharmacognosist in Kennebunk, he recommended Cindy Angerhofer.

Meantime, the board, deep into our strategic planning for the future of the company, was concerned that by veering off into pharmacognosy, we might lose our focus on our primary business, which was oral care. I countered that such a move from our core business of personal care to addressing our customers' total wellness was a logical next step for Tom's of Maine. My presentation even included a graphic argument: a picture of a tree whose trunk was the company's mission, planted in soil and society, and branching off were our new natural products, skin care, pet care, and natural remedies. I argued that the company would use what we learned from plants and herbs first to strengthen our basic personal care products with antimicrobials and antioxidants from plants, make our line more interesting with pharmacognosy, and then move into herbal supplements, first aid, natural therapies, and so on. Board member Paul Duffley noted that he was on the board of the American Health Foundation, the foremost researcher on antioxidants, and suggested we meet with them. With the help of American Health, we are now developing an antioxidant recipe for mouthwash and toothpaste that would give us a product that would help strengthen the immune system of your oral cavity so that your gums would be healthier. It was the kind of solution that we had been unable to find, a natural way to protect the mouth and gums that didn't have to kill bacteria.

The board got what I was trying to do. But they also knew that the company did not have the people to pull it off. I suggested that we create a scientific advisory board made up of experts in antioxidants and pharmacognosy. I knocked on the door of Cindy Angerhofer's ex-boss, the head of the pharmacognosy department at the University of Illinois at Chicago, Norman Farnsworth, who is not only a premier authority on medicinal plants but also operates an elaborate database for natural products that includes all the clinical studies done in the world on a particular herb or plant. After a couple of hours of listening to the salesman from Maine, he agreed to become a scientific advisor to the company. He also put us onto Steven Foster, an authority on herbal remedies based in Arkansas who happened to have once lived in Maine, and Fred Siegel, a pharmacist skilled at taking a pharmacognosist's prescription and turning those natural ingredients into a product that would actually work.

Thus we created a whole new circle of advisors, a new group of professionals. We knew we needed them, but why did they want to work with us? After all, Tom's of Maine is hardly the first to get into the natural medicine business; hundreds of companies are making this move, including some of the biggest in the nation. Norman Farnsworth could have advised us not to bother. Instead, he told us that the reason he and others were interested in working with Tom's of Maine was that ''your name stands for something. And that is what the customer wants.''

WHEN YOU HAVE ADVISORS, TAKE THEIR ADVICE

When I first began thinking about expanding into natural therapies, I was considering only Chinese medicine. But now that I had an herbalist, a pharmacognosist, a scientist, and a market researcher who really understood how to ask consumers what they thought about emerging ideas and new therapies from natural medicine, I decided to run my idea past them. I sought the advice of family members who had a lifelong interest in plants and medicinals. I also wanted to hear from lawyers and other businessmen experienced in dealing with the FDA. All of these different perspectives opened us up to considering not just the traditional medical practices of one culture but of the whole world.

If I had been an impulsive, arrogant CEO (indeed, the man I used to be), I might have hung my hat on Chinese medicine alone. Instead, I benefited from a wide-ranging circle of perspectives, enriched my understanding of the field of natural medicine, and in the process found a number of world-class professionals who could help Tom's of Maine create a new business in a smart and responsible way. We will take from Chinese traditions, but we will also learn from Indian cultures as well as Native American and Western European traditions. At the same time, we will have to deal with a myriad of issues related to the FDA, which disapproves of the kind of combinations of herb extracts that exist in the natural medicines of some cultures and have the imprimatur of government regulators in other countries. Initially, we will probably have to limit ourselves to single herb products, like echinacea, the natural cold remedy, St. John's wort, the herbal antidepressive, and saw palmetto, which has a richly documented effect on benign prostate enlargement, a common problem among men as they age.

Launching a new business comprising literally a world of medicines is bound to be difficult and complex. But that's the challenge of it, and indeed its beauty.

FINALLY, THE BUCK STOPS HERE

An Upside Down company will thrive on outside advice and creative solutions from its staff. But no business can be a pure democracy. The buck must stop somewhere; someone is responsible for the final decision. Power resides in every one of the eighty-five people who work on the management side of Tom's of Maine. *Authority*, however, is differentiated in a hierarchical system of finer and finer accountability according to particular roles. For instance, our explorations into the new natural wellness business have passed through a cascade of authority from the owners of the company to the board of directors to officers to managers and beyond, to the company's scientific advisory board. As owner, CEO, and the progenitor of the move into this new area—as the champion of this new product acorn—I will be making many of the final decisions. To be sure, they will be difficult decisions, but by the time I have to make them, so many people will have weighed in, so many shared decisions will already have been made, that my decisions will reflect the wisdom of the group. In the end, I will agree, edit, or disagree. I will not give up the authority to run the process, but I will benefit from the group's advice, and the group will own the final result.

To make such decisions, I seek out another kind of advice—from myself. By reflecting on everything I've heard and read, by reviewing all the preliminary information, research, and decisions, I can reach the point where I am comfortable making a final decision. One of my teachers in divinity school, Professor Richard Niebuhr, once said that the purpose of education at a place like Harvard was to create a "reflective citizen." Reflection also has a place in the world of business, and I wish more business executives realized it. Instead, we are controlled by our agendas. Each day, a list of things to do and decide appears on our desk, and we discuss them, make our decisions, and move on to the next thing on the agenda. It is as if there is nothing more to say about these issues until review time.

We often miss out on the wisdom of our own moral imagination, that deeper part of our being that is talking back to us about the positions we've already taken in public. In traditional business relationships between a superior and a subordinate, you're expected to grasp the situation, process the information, and make a decision. There is little time for reflection. When seeking advice, however, you're listening, thinking rationally, and reflecting on how all of this fits into the bigger picture, which includes your values. To step away from the fray and spend some time in reflection is to allow your moral imagination, the source of your deepest fundamental values, to weigh in.

To make a big decision, I find that I need somewhere between twenty-four and forty-eight hours for effective reflection on the substantive issues involved. If I am making a decision or giving an answer to someone who wants to go ahead on a particular project, I make the decision in private, and if it gnaws at me, if it gives me some discomfort, I review it overnight. With so many things going on in my personal, family, and business lives, I have learned that I need a couple of days' reflection to feel really comfortable with a tough decision. After reflection, I may even decide that I need some time to talk about the issues some more. Working with my new partner, Tom O'Brien, I have found that in three-hour blocks of time, we can accomplish an awful lot. Nevertheless, some topics have required more reflection. We have decided to respect the nature of reflection as a normal aspect of our responsibility, and we have begun integrating substantial reflection time for both of us into our working relationship. That doesn't mean that we are going back on what we are inclined to do; it just recognizes the fact that just because an issue comes up on the agenda does not mean that it's ready to be decided. Every decision needs its own time.

That is the difference between analysis and wisdom.

ONE OTHER SOURCE OF WISDOM—GOD

I also take time out to pray. Every morning, I get on my knees and pray. It's how I keep in touch with my sense of goodness in the world, which for me is God. That kind of prayer is as much a part of my daily routine as brushing my teeth. But there is another kind of prayer for the times when I'm up against it and need advice.

During that five-month period when Kate and I were exploring selling the company, I found myself praying a lot for the wisdom to recognize God's will. A typical day was spent meeting with our attorneys about how to set up charitable foundations so that my family would have ways of channeling our new wealth into the kinds of philanthropy we cared about. I spent time identifying all the organizations and institutions we were going to give money to. I spent time worrying about my income and whether it would be sufficient for both my lifestyle and philanthropy. What about maximizing my tax advantages? Then there was the question of who my investment advisors would be. Suddenly it was time to have a meeting with our employees to update them on our efforts to find the right buyer for the company. "What am I supposed to do about the mortgage application I just filed?" asks one of the employees. "When you sell the company, will I still have a job?"

I found myself praying for the answers to all of those questions. What my gut was telling me was that I was going to find maintaining wealth a very boring job. Clipping coupons was not my thing. Meantime, my heart was going out to that guy who was losing sleep over that mortgage application. I began looking back on my life and realized that what I had enjoyed most was creating wealth, not maintaining it.

I realized that this was God talking to me. When you pray to know God's will on huge life issues such as selling the company that has dominated your life for almost three decades, you don't get an e-mail in return. Nor are you likely to hear a voice in the night instructing you what to do. When you're praying to have the proper mindset to make a big decision, you have to pay attention to the signs. Such prayer is a kind of personal inquiry. You are facing a big decision, and like any decision, you gather the relevant data to make it. Among that data is your own sense of what is right. After a lot of thought and prayer and taking notice of the signs, Kate and I decided against selling. It was a huge decision, but we made it, and have never looked back.

SOME PRACTICAL ADVICE FOR GETTING ADVICE
Over the years, I have learned that the quickest way to a diverse group of opinions is to set up a circle of people with different back-

grounds and interests. As I mentioned in Chapter 2, the talking circle is a device we borrowed from the Native Americans to inspire modern business managers to listen to one another and solve problems together. Conference tables inevitably banish some people to the far end of the conversation; the office desk can easily become an intimidating physical (and psychological) barrier.

At Tom's of Maine, we literally create a circle of chairs, set the topic, and invite everyone's opinions. Assembling in a circle immediately democratizes the group; everyone has an equal position. The circle also underscores the interdependence of the company. The circle can take the idea of one person and make it the group's idea. Everyone can contribute to the creative process and the planning of strategies, and everyone has his or her role. Thus we have tried to inspire diversity by letting the diversity of a Native American tradition inspire us.

Even our consumer mail is representative of a kind of circle between the company and its customers. Our package outserts and inserts give information and invite a reply. We get fifteen thousand letters a year, and the contents, good or bad, are often sent to the appropriate departments; answers are sent back to the customer, completing the circle.

But you have to listen. The best advice in the world is useless unless you prove you really want it by listening and acting. I remember several years ago writing a business plan, presenting it to the board, and asking for feedback. I heard nothing. I went to the psychologist on the board, Pearl Rutledge, and asked her why. She frankly explained that I was an intimidating force when I was full of energy for a particular idea or plan. "You've got to remember that people don't know how to come back at you, to disagree with you on a point of strategy, because they are afraid that you won't listen." Surprised, I told her that I didn't want to put this plan out in a vacuum. I had a board because I wanted to hear from them. Pearl candidly informed me that I would have to convince the board that I really did want to hear their side. She suggested that I revise my way of communicating by beginning with something like, "I've got this idea for a plan. Here is what I think about it, but I really want to know what you think about it." She also suggested that I follow up with phone calls emphasizing that I wanted to know what they thought about my plan. "I want you to exaggerate to the point where people feel free to give you their advice."

I have never forgotten what Pearl told me, and I pass it along to you: Throw your ideas on the table for comment, and then try to bury your inclination to be defensive by showing your enthusiasm for new ideas and constructive criticism. You have brought these people together because they know something you do not; take advantage of their expertise. Encourage disagreement among your managers and other employees. For the past decade, I have tried to engender more autonomy among my employees in their daily decision-making. The goal was to cancel out the first response of most employees: What will the boss think? I remember complaining to another board member, Ruth Purtillo, an ethicist, that people weren't taking the liberty I offered them to step beyond the obvious and try to imagine different solutions. She pointed out to me that "it is easy to be creative and expansive when you're at the top of the pyramid." She advised me to "create an environment in which they feel free to disagree, where they can give you their passions, and where they know that they will not be fired for making mistakes." That advice helped me see that no matter how open and democratic I try to be, I will always be different within my company because I own the place. If I want to blow it up, it's okay, but if anyone else tried to do the same, it would not be so okay.

Advice is all around you—all you have to do is ask. I'm forever finding people on planes or on the other side of the telephone line who can help me. I like to compare it to asking someone out on a date. You want to, but you're scared to make the call because you're sure you'll be rejected. But you'll never get to first base unless you try. Take my advice: People who know their subject are not only eager to discuss it, but are flattered by your interest. In my experience, you ask someone an intelligent question, and the information will flow your way.

As we moved forward with our plans for the Tom's of Maine Natural Wellness Center, one of my consultants suggested that we needed an M.D. to round out the scientific advisory board. Busy with other matters, I hadn't really given it much thought. Then one day last year, I was sitting in a plane, traveling from Florida back to Maine, when I noticed that the man in the seat next to me was reading a book on herbs. Consumed by the subject for months, I couldn't resist interrupting him. We began talking, and I learned that he was an oncologist returning from the annual National Institutes of Health meeting on cancer research. He said he was interested in herbal medicine and tried to keep up on the literature. I told him about what I did and our plans to move into natural medicines. Amazingly, he was not only a fan of Tom's of Maine products but had graduated from the same college I had, Trinity in Hartford. As we were about to land, I wondered whether he'd be interested in another conversation. "Sure," he said. "I think what you're planning to do is a great idea."

I went into the office the next morning and announced, "I've found the M.D.!" "Where?" asked Tom O'Brien. "On the plane," I said, proving once again that advice is everywhere. Dr. John Grous joined us for the next meeting of the scientific advisory board, giving us a cancer specialist's take on the medicinal effects of plants and herbs. It was just what we needed.

TOM'S OF MAINE'S ADVISOR-IN-CHIEF

Neither of us will ever forget the first day we met. Anxious to make a positive impression on a senior partner of one of the world's most esteemed management consulting firms and to assure him that he wasn't dealing with some Maine hippie, I dressed in my best gray flannel Brooks Brothers suit. The senior vice president and director of the Manhattan-based firm of Booz Allen & Hamilton, who has a home at Kennebunk Beach, showed up in his L.L. Bean boots and rain slicker. "I looked at this tall, good-looking picture from Brooks Brothers," Rock recalls, "and said, 'Goodness gracious! Who's the New Yorker here!'" A Harvard MBA, John R. Rockwell spent the last seventeen years of his career with Booz Allen in various management positions before retiring in 1990. Good for him and all the better for Tom's of Maine, because retirement for Rock means a little golf, boating in Florida, spending time with his three grandchildren, and being free to indulge his interest in entrepreneurial companies like Tom's of Maine that are, in his words, "doing good as well as doing well." John Rockwell is one of those rare business pros who have long understood the importance of values. He credits five people in his life for pointing him in the direction of values-oriented management. Four of those people he met in the business world. The fifth is his wife of forty-seven years, Lorraine. "Let's face it, people are trained at Harvard Business School to be takers, not givers," he explains. "Lorraine taught me the value of giving." The value of Rock's experience and keen business mind have been incalculable to Tom's of Maine. He's a man who knows how to use his head and his heart.

And no one knows better how tough it has been to give Tom Chappell advice.

Over the years, Tom has become much more pragmatic than when he was first testing the hypothesis of his brand of socially responsible capitalism. I think he's much more relaxed about his ideas, particularly in terms of the give-and-take, more open to criticism and advice. He used to be more inflexible, much more convinced that for Tom's of Maine, only the views of Tom should prevail.

Exploring the sale of the company was an interesting example of how Tom has grown in this respect. I helped him draw up the offering document for the investment bankers. We were very hard-nosed about there being both a social value and commercial value in this property, and any prospective buyer would have to buy into both acts, so to speak. This wasn't simply saying, "Let's sell the company and take the toothpaste production down to North Carolina." We decided not to compromise the values of the company; they were inviolate in the truest sense of the word. Quite frankly, nobody placed any value on our values. That still boggles my mind. But given that fact, then what? Tom sought out my advice, and I advised that we had to find him a partner to be the COO of the company. "You don't want to fight in the swamp anymore," I told him. "You shouldn't have to." He had other interests, teaching entrepreneurship, conveying values-centered leadership, and creating a foundation to do that.

But the notion of taking on a partner was a very hard idea for him to grasp intellectually. I understood why, because Tom's of Maine was at the stage of what we call a "threshold company"—that is, an entrepreneurial company that gets to the threshold of being something more and never crosses over to the next stage. Generally, the roadblock is not the idea of the business; it's the individual entrepreneur who can't let go. The entrepreneur is inclined to say, "That's not the way I do things." Entrepreneurs classically have trouble understanding that what they did to make a company happen is not necessarily the same thing required to make it grow. I have worked with a lot of those companies, fascinating companies, and I saw what Tom was doing: He had institutionalized in his own mind his approach to business. It was difficult for him to accept another way. I suspect that changing the trademark from "Tom's" to "Tom's of Maine" in 1980 helped. Also, the fact that the company became perceived and then accepted as a high-values kind of an institution in the marketplace. Important, too, is that the spirit of the times has caught up with Tom's of Maine. We are in an era of not only values, but spirituality, too, has become an issue in the workplace. All sorts of people are eager to hear Tom speak. If you believe there's a set of customers out there who share the values of Tom's of Maine—distributors of our products and consumers—then there's a meaningful way to differentiate this company, which I think extends beyond the flavor or efficacy of, say, a toothpaste . . .

What Tom's of Maine has created is brand equity. It has become a standard for "natural." I think it has the potential to not only be the standard, but also make a difference in terms of values-centered value . . . But Tom's of Maine is still a company in transition. Years ago, I said to Tom, "Let's see if we can earn the right to be successful. Let's figure out how to do that." Now that we've just about got there, we have to see if we can earn the right to make a difference. We've gotten big enough to be successful, but we're not quite yet big enough to make a difference. We're on the verge of almost being big enough to start to make a difference, but we're still not quite there. These two goals are, of course, linked. The more successful a company becomes, the more meaningful Tom's view of the world becomes. But it's a subtle balance. If you become too preachy or values-driven, then you risk confusing the marketplace in terms of the value of the product itself. We have to capture a subtle trade-off between the business we're in and the values we promote.

That's why a new person like Tom O'Brien is so crucial. He has a rare combination of experience; he came from an entrepreneurial family with solid values, went to Harvard Business School, and, more important, learned his lessons well and successfully at Procter & Gamble. He got Tom's of Maine immediately—that the company was not about selling tubes of toothpaste, it was about selling ''goodness.'' More important for the growth of this company, O'Brien could intellectualize that distinction and then, using his P&G experience, put it into a sophisticated marketing framework. What Tom O'Brien brings is what I have long argued that we needed, a kind of next-generation founder of Tom's of Maine, someone who can take it from an entrepreneur's company that could not function without Tom Chappell to an entrepreneurial company with someone who can partner both intellectually and operationally with Tom.

We're now ready to cross the threshold, and that is a testament to Tom's ability to seek advice, and, more important, to take it to heart.

INTENTION #4 TALKING POINTS

Everyone makes mistakes, and the best protection against such mistakes is seeking the advice of other people.

Knowledge is power, and true knowledge comes from a variety of sources—including failure.

Essential to Managing Upside Down is recognizing that wisdom can reside outside the boss's office.

Potential advisors are all around you.

Seek out the counsel of experts. They will be happy to help, and usually for free.

Set up an advisory board.

Listen to them.

Seeking advice creates a richer outcome.

INTENTION #4 HOMEWORK

With this Intention, you step away from yourself and ask others how you're doing. Before we begin, write this down and paste it over your workspace: "I don't have to do this by myself."

Based on your vision of the destiny you worked on in the last chapter—your vision statement—write a letter to a close friend about your life—as if it were ten years from now. Assume that everything has gone according to your dreams. Make this letter as vivid as you can, including all your achievements, promotions, triumphs, honors, etc.

Read this letter to a friend or family member, and ask:

- What seemed to you to be most important to me?
- If you had my vision, what would be the images you would have included in your letter?
- What are the three things you liked most about what I wrote?

- What was the one thing that concerned you most about my account of this ten-year period?

After this exercise, write down the answers to these questions:

- How did it feel to share your letter?
- What was it like to listen to someone else's advice?
- What more do you now know about your vision as a result of this exercise?
- How did this exercise help you articulate this vision of your destiny?

List the people in your life whom you think of as wise.

Check off the three people you would most like to seek advice from who would be willing to help. Now strategize for making it happen.

- How will you approach these people?
- When will you meet them?
- What exactly do you want from them?

Now bounce this plan off someone else and listen to his or her take on your strategy. Revise your vision accordingly.

7

Venture Out

Build a creative strategy for every dimension of your new business, make sure it is aligned with your values, and go for it— even if there is nothing like it in the world.

I remember a dinner party at my home almost twenty years ago when a guest picked up a package of our cocoa orange soap and got everyone in the room's attention with his big booming voice, asking, "Where's the benefit in this product?" He was a senior marketing executive at a large European packaged goods company, and he thought he knew what a package was supposed to say. "I'm looking at the label," he announced, "and it doesn't tell me what this soap will do for me." I asked him to tell us what the package actually said. "Tom's of Maine's Cocoa-Orange Soap," he replied. "And then it tells me what's in the product."

That was precisely the Tom's of Maine difference. I pointed out to him that we were not selling soap; we were selling *natural* ingredients, and the information on the package, front and back, listed those ingredients and explained where they came from and what their benefits were. We were in the business of serving customers eager for a lifestyle that was in harmony with nature and protected the environment. That commitment to nature was what set us apart.

It was a message that was not even obvious to us at the start. The market kept telling us we were in the soap or the toothpaste business, and it took us years and a fair amount of internecine battles before we hit upon what our role really was, a personal care company that specialized in natural ingredients. We spent the next decade selling "natural" only to realize that what we were really selling were our values. Customers were trying our products, we discovered, not just because they wanted a natural toothpaste or deodorant, but because they shared our values and liked what we were doing for the environment and the community. We realized that we were selling values as well as a very effective line of natural personal care products.

And now we are taking another leap into space to become a values-driven company that aims to serve a customer's total personal care and wellness needs with natural products. How do you get from toothpaste to cough syrup? How do you get from soap to an antioxidant elixir that you can take every morning? From shampoo to echinacea lozenges for your cold? You dream, you create, you plan, and you take a risk—that's how you reinvigorate a company and keep growing. With your values backing you up, with years of trust from loyal customers to bank on, you are willing to go even to where no one else has ever gone. *You venture out.*

Venturing out is coming forward with a creative plan that is consistent with your values, who you are, and where you are going on your journey. It is an exciting time when the imagination and the give-and-take conversation between you, your advisors, and your employees come together into new creative thinking and action. Ventures usually take you off on a new route to do something in a way different from how it has been done before.

In our case, we have always headed into the unknown with a concept and not an economic model, as most companies do. You have to help everyone in the company understand that you are in the business of creating natural solutions for customers who are oriented toward nature. You are not limited to any particular product or business because you have customers who already trust you and are willing to try just about anything you send their way. How you finance the idea comes next, and there, too, you must be creative. Maybe you go to venture capitalists. But then they might not be interested in a company driven by values in general, or your kind of values. Or if they give you the money, they might demand it back so quickly that you will be under too much pressure to pull off your new strategy. You can turn to friends or to the Small Business Administration (a wonderful source of working capital for us, incidentally). You must also consider your potential market—everybody, or just those people who are likely to want what you have to sell. Tom's of Maine made a decision very early in the game that we did not see every adult in the world as a potential customer; instead, we focused on those who shared our respect for other people, the community, and the environment.

CREATING SOMETHING OUT OF CHAOS

Venturing out is the culmination of a process. Once you've placed your values at the center of your business, set some goals, thought about them, came up with plans to get there, analyzed what was already out there in the marketplace, and sought advice, you may realize that what you are doing is still chaotic. Part of the venturing-out process is to shape this chaos. The other essential is knowing that you cannot pull this off by yourself. Venturing out is a collaborative process. A precondition is creating a team, that circle of people with particular experiences and skills relevant to the task at hand. Once you have your team, you have to give its members the opportunity to imagine out loud where you want to go. Creativity is often a fusion of opposites, different ideas emerging from the circle, a single imagination building on that idea, the conversation that emits the "ah-ha!" when someone puts the final piece of the puzzle in place and the picture suddenly becomes clear.

Venturing out puts together creativity and risk-taking. Once you've found the solution to what once seemed an insoluble problem, the conversation must turn to what to do next. It is too easy to go on talking forever, exploring the finer points of who you are, what values you care about, and your destiny. Finally, venturing out is about trying something, taking a flier. What's the goal? When do we start? What's the deadline? Who's responsible?

MAKING IT BIG OFTEN REQUIRES A BIG LEAP

It is a risky business, this venturing out. It often requires you to transform your business into something so new that it's never been done before. Reinventing your business can feel awkward and uncomfortable; sometimes it can feel like stepping into an abyss.

Like when I had the idea to go into the toothpaste business. Back in the 1970s, our company was called Tom's Natural Soaps. We were selling a nonpolluting laundry detergent, a natural cocoa-orange liquid soap, and an apple shampoo. I thought we should go into the natural personal care business and began exploring possible products that we could do naturally, including toothpaste. Exploring the contents of the various brands of toothpaste on the shelves, I began wondering whether I should be putting this stuff in my mouth. I couldn't really find any brand that provided a friendly set of ingredients; they were filled with additives, dyes, and artificial sweeteners. I asked my chemist, Blaine Tewksbury, if we could come up with a toothpaste made from natural ingredients. ''Sure,'' he said, and we began discussing what we could put in such a product. This was a new world for our company, and he and I became explorers.

We met with resistance from Kate and others in the company concerned that we were venturing too far afield. What did we know about toothpaste? Nothing. But we would learn. Through my persistence, we eventually developed a toothpaste in the lab using 100 percent natural ingredients. When I was finally able to hand some samples around the office, people said, ''Well, gee, this is pretty good.'' I noted that it was all natural, showing them the ingredients in the brands on the market. "Does getting into the natural toothpaste business make sense to you?" I got a yes all around, and we proceeded to get the product ready to go to market.

When I started talking to our health food store distributors and retailers about our natural toothpaste, they, too, resisted. They thought that their customers would be more interested in natural cosmetic products for their skin and hair than toothpaste. Nevertheless, we put our natural toothpaste on the market, and it was an instant success. Soon the company, which had been known for its soaps and shampoos, became a "toothpaste company." Today, oral care is 80 percent of our business.

So venture out and explore the far reaches of your imagination because, well, you never know.

Like when we decided to take our products mass market. Everyone warned how risky it would be to try to compete with the biggest companies on the planet. Some were worried that we would antagonize the very people who had made us a success, the health food stores, who tend to guard their products jealously. In my mind, however, we weren't competing against the giants or biting the hand that had fed us; we were going to put the same label—Tom's of Maine—into both kinds of stores for one reason only: There were ten times as many customers who shopped in supermarkets and drugstores rather than health food stores who were interested in natural products. I knew my health food storeowners would be annoyed because in the past the health food store products that crossed over to the supermarkets were usually sold for less. Once I had the interest of the chain stores, I visited our key natural food distributors with a flip chart in hand, showing them a graphic of how I intended to serve them and what I intended to do over and above that relationship in order to build my business. At the time, supermarkets were calling natural food distributors to help them set up "health food" sections in their stores. I told the health food people that I didn't want to be in some specialty section; I wanted to be on the toothpaste shelf. I also told them that I wouldn't be discounting my price for the big boys. They laughed at me and sent me on my way. But they continued to do business with me because I had been forthright about telling them my plans.

By going mass market, Tom's of Maine was able to build a business with three times the potential we had in health food stores. The added volume enabled us to afford an advertising budget to get the word out. We saw not the retailers but the consumers as our customers, and to serve them we would have to be in the stores where they shopped.

It was a legitimate thing to do, but it was also risky to declare our independence from our health food mentors. We took a flyer, and it was a defining moment for the company. Today, our business is probably three parts mass market to one part health food stores. But we have hardly abandoned the health food trade; on the contrary, we have grown that segment of the business at a double-digit rate every year since we made the decision to expand.

MY LATEST VENTURE

Looking back, I realize that the company has reinvented itself no less than five times. Over the course of almost three decades now, we've gone from essentially a hippie soap company to an international player in personal care and wellness. The goal of our most recent metamorphosis—the entry into herbal medicines—is to bring to the marketplace something that is not there that will contribute to people's wellness.

Once again, we began not with a financial model but with a concept. To explore this new idea for a business, we put together a special team of nine Tom's of Maine people, including me and Tom O'Brien, plus three outsiders, the pharmacognosist Norman Farnsworth, the herbalist Steven Foster, plus our graphics designer, Rod Williams, who could give us a picture of a possible product on the spot. We are creating products unlike any we've ever done before; we are going inside the body itself. Are we anxious? You bet. A lot of other companies have already moved into this herbal business.

But we believe we have a major advantage: Tom's of Maine is one of the most trusted names in the natural products industry.

The board and I agreed that we would have to immerse ourselves in the field. The consultants we had brought in would get us up to speed on the science. But we also had to research how extractors, growers, and formulators worked in China, India, and Germany. There were regulatory issues. In China, for example, they make blends of herbs. In the U.S., the FDA requires you to defend your claims for each individual drug in the formula. If you do not have clinical evidence that a combination of certain herbs is the optimal formulation, then your only recourse is to come out with a product made from only one of the herbs.

Once we got a handle on all those issues, we had a two-day venturing-out session to brainstorm about new products. To make it fun, we broke into two groups, each with a set of symptoms to inspire the group members to envision a product (e.g., a cold, a cough, indigestion, constipation, depression, etc.). We had a ball as people played the roles of patients, consulting physicians, and pharmacists. During these two days of teaming up, imagining, dialoguing, and creating, we developed concepts and simple graphics for six new personal care products and forty-five new ones in the wellness area. At the time, Tom's of Maine was selling only twenty-seven products in varieties of sizes and flavors.

The next step was the hard science. We had to get our formulation chemists involved. The first product we developed was a decongestant with lemon and ginger. We had gone from the idea stage— "Hey, let's have a natural decongestant!"—to learning what ingredients should go into such a product, why, and where they should come from. Then came the moment of truth when Fred Siegel, our consulting pharmacist, walked out of the lab with a little bottle and passed it around the room for us to try. I'll never forget taking that teaspoon of cough syrup with lemon and ginger and the feeling of it rushing through my body. I knew we had done it. Up to then, it had been all smoke and queasy stomachs.

We were in business—the wellness business, which meant, suddenly, that there were a lot of business questions to answer. Where would our ingredients come from? Who would grow the plants and herbs? What factories would do the extractions of the biologically active substances from the plants? What would the packaging look like, and what kind of claims would we make on it? Our usual customers and retailers were out there, and we would have to educate them. We'd also have to reach out to physicians and pharmacists. Clearly, this would be too much for one person to do. The twelve of us were on the verge of burnout. But we've never done anything as exciting. Twenty-five years of experience in developing personal care products came together in this new venture.

And then we had an epiphany: We could wrap all our products, our existing personal care line and these new plant and herbal ideas, under one umbrella—a "Tom's of Maine Natural Wellness Center" that we could design as one location in the stores for all of Tom's of Maine's products. The room went silent as people tried to take in the notion of combining what seemed to be two different businesses, each with its own expectations, risks, and requirements. All through this creative process, we had viewed the herbal business as something new and distinct from our personal care products. Suddenly we began to see both as part of one bigger, more complex business. The Tom's of Maine Natural Wellness Center would become a way through which we could serve our customers' total wellness needs. We soon realized that the herbal business would bring more customers into contact with our personal care products.

Venturing out is scary. Whether you are painting a picture, writing a book, throwing a pot at the wheel, or dreaming up a new concept for a product, you are injecting yourself into that moment of creation. By venturing out, you are risking your wisdom and thus the most intimate part of your self. If you offer a new idea and someone stops you out of the box, you will certainly be slow to offer it again. Warning: The world is full of people lying in wait to tell you that your ideas are stupid. Most companies do not allow their employees to let their imaginations run free. Creativity is constantly censored.

The Upside Down Manager recognizes that his greatest creative resource is his people. The more ideas, the better the results. More important, the muse of creativity does not discriminate according to gender, age, race, or religious affiliation.

WANTED: NEW IDEAS, NO EXPERIENCE NECESSARY

We had an idea for a new business. Great. We had some of the best minds in the nation on our team helping us dream up products. Terrific. We would put all our products under one umbrella, the Tom's of Maine Natural Wellness Center. Brilliant. But at the time, we were selling only twenty-seven products. We now had to figure out how to market more than twice that number that were not in our customary personal care category.

That was truly scary. Where would we put them in the stores? Surely we couldn't put three Tom's of Maine products into the cold/cough section and eight into the herbal supplement aisle. Even if we could persuade the stores to do it, we'd be virtually invisible. I came up with a solution: We would create one merchandising space for all the Tom's of Maine products, our current line of natural soaps, deodorants, mouthwash, and toothpastes plus the new herbal wellness products, a Tom's of Maine Natural Wellness Center kiosk that could first be positioned in large commercial spaces, like an airport or in the middle of a mall. The hope was that a public kiosk would be so successful that our retailers would want a smaller version for their stores. For tinier stores, we would supply a Tom's of Maine Natural Wellness Center "endcap," one of those special displays you find at the end of the aisle at your supermarket or drugstore chain featuring that week's special or discounted item.

That was creative. It was certainly the Upside Down way of marketing products. But could we actually pull it off? Tom O'Brien and I created a "Kiosks Initiative." I then made the controversial decision to put my twenty-three-year-old daughter Eliza in charge of it.

We were taking a huge leap into space, and I needed someone who got what we were up to. Eliza, though a relative newcomer to the company, had a combination of talents unique to the company: She had worked in retailing before high school as a salesclerk in a clothing store, has a great eye for design, is very intuitive about interaction with customers, and is a born entrepreneur. She had already done a fine job leading a team effort to design our first mail order catalogue. I knew that with some help from Tom O'Brien and me, she could choose and head up an in-house design team that could work with an outside team of designers who specialized in these kinds of kiosk displays. And while older, more experienced managers in the marketing department might be annoyed, there were plenty of precedents where the company had empowered people because of their skills and talent, regardless of their youth.

Immediately we ran into another roadblock on the kiosk project. The outside design team advised going with the simplest display first, the endcap. We preferred beginning with the biggest challenge because we were convinced that if the mall kiosks worked, retailers would be more likely to install smaller versions in their stores. It seemed the more creative solution. When you're perceived as a company in the toothpaste business, you have to do something striking to get the market to notice you're making a move in a new direction. The big kiosks, we figured, would get the word out pretty fast. Eliza began working with graphic designer Rod Williams on the various designs.

Getting the right design turned out to be a lot harder than we thought. Eliza's team proposed various possibilities, and none, we all agreed, seemed to have everything we needed. We brainstormed about what we wanted and didn't want, and we stumbled from one design to another. But we could not seem to get down on paper a design that inspired us all to say, "This is it!" And I was not going to go into construction before we had a kiosk that we were fired up about. I decided to bring in a new eye, Scott Teas, an architect who had done work for our family and for the company. At first, it seemed outrageous for us to reach out into the world of architecture for a store display. But hiring an architect turned out to be the missing piece of the puzzle. Scott's skill at translating concepts into actual structures, partnered with the Kiosk Initiative Team's clear sense of Tom's of Maine's move from toothpaste company to one serving the total wellness needs of our customers, produced a design that struck us as right.

We decided to use the kiosk design as the basis for a 600-square-foot exhibit at the Health Food Trade Show in Anaheim, California, in March 1999, where the company introduced its new wellness business. The result was stunning. Under the umbrella of Tom's of Maine Natural Wellness Center are five stations, featuring all our products. A customer can move from station to station, sampling all our new products, from the baking soda mouthwash to an echinacea tonic. In the middle of the structure is the "Tom's of Maine Institute of Pharmacognosy" that explains our recent commitment to research in the science of pharmacognosy. The exhibit is a beautiful thing, the embodiment of oral, body, and internal wellness with natural medicinals that we are embracing under the Tom's of Maine Natural Wellness Center umbrella. Every fixture is made of wood and other natural materials.

The success of the kiosk design was classic Managing Upside Down. The authority came from me and Tom O'Brien to turn a dream into a reality. The right creative people came together, including outside vendors, and this special team made it happen. We moved from vision to execution to an actual 20-by-30-foot kiosk exhibit—and without sacrificing a dollar or a principle. Above all, the design announces that what you are looking at is a new company.

DON'T BE AFRAID TO BREAK THE MOLD (OR INVENT A NEW ONE)

I have learned many things about life and business from my co-founder and wife, Kate, but the lesson that is on my mind most during these days of new beginnings is that business can be an art (see box on p. 141). What most businesses do is mimic the competition; they check out what's selling, keep an eye out for trends, and then churn out their version of what's working best in the marketplace. It's comparable to the TV networks trying to clone last year's most popular shows, forgetting that the shows were a hit because they were different from everything else that was on. That's not creativity; it's imitation.

To stand apart from the herd, particularly when you're a small company, you have to be creative. No matter how many brilliant products we dream up, Tom's of Maine risks being relegated to a fraction of a shelf filled with the products of our bigger, richer, and better-known competitors. We will be just one more brand, and a tiny one at that. But if we create Tom's of Maine Natural Wellness Center kiosks so that the on-the-go consumer can see all our different products in one place, then we're not just one more brand, we're a store within a store.

In a business like ours, dominated by huge international companies, Tom's of Maine can hardly compete by outspending our competitors; our advertising budget is minuscule, our sales staff modest. But creativity has nothing to do with size or budget. We simply have to reinvent ourselves and find innovative ways of doing business.

CREATING A NEW WAY OF DOING BUSINESS

When Tom O'Brien first joined the company, he spent a day in a health food store meeting people, and then he spent the next day with a mass-market team. He was surprised by the difference. Kate and I had built relationships with the health food trade based on their beliefs and values, which happened to be our beliefs and values. In the mass market, however, what counted was the product. No one bothered discussing a company's values. He wanted to change that, according to our mission "to build a relationship with our customers that extends beyond product usage to include full and honest dialogue, responsive to feedback, and the exchange of information about product and issues." Tom thought that we needed to come up with some specific new strategies that reflected our values.

It is another example of venturing out. "I wanted to provide an environment that would allow our partners to experience us as health food store owners used to experience you and Kate in the early days," he told me. "They were able to get a sense of who you were and what you believed in instead of just being handed a deal sheet." So we took two very important accounts, Whole Foods and Wild Oats, and said to them that in order to improve our ongoing dialogue and to understand both our needs, we would like to form a multi-functional team with representatives from both companies (i.e., from finance, sales, and consumer development; one team for each account). Such diversity, we hoped, would create a genuine dialogue between the companies instead of having one salesperson talking to one buyer. The goal was for all of us to understand the other company. If you had asked four people from the Whole Foods sales department, for example, "What is important to you about the mission of Whole Foods?" you would have gotten four different answers. "If you were to ask the same four people today, after they've served on these joint teams, each would give you the same answer," says Tom O'Brien. "And as their partners, Tom's of Maine really understands the needs of Whole Foods in a very holistic way and in its entirety." Equally as important, if you ask people at Whole Foods, from the president down, what Tom's of Maine is up to in serving customers' needs, they know because they understand our beliefs and values. As companies, we are interacting around those values to serve their shoppers *together*. "This common understanding of one another and our mission to serve consumer needs has been remarkable," says Tom O'Brien, emphasizing that it could never have happened without the two sides meeting face to face over eight months. "It's not something that you can do just once, and it's all set up," Tom explains. "That shared face-to-face time over several months is the fuel that builds relationships. You cannot do it over the phone or by mail or through a deal sheet. The beauty of it is that this operationalizes the mission of the company. It's no longer just words but action."

And Tom Chappell does not have to be there. Our values are clear enough. Better still, such partnerships reduce hierarchy. The first time the intercompany team met, the person who perceived himself as the highest-ranking member of the group tried to take charge. Another member of the group called time-out and said, "I was under the assumption that when we came together there was no hierarchy here." During the second meeting, a couple of vice presidents approached Tom O'Brien outside the meeting to ask his opinion on what the team should do. "Do you have permission from the team to be talking to me?" Tom asked. He and the rest of the team had agreed up front that the goal of the meetings was to build relations between the two sides and achieve a kind of diversity in their relationships with customers. "I told them to go away and ask themselves whether they were achieving the mutually agreed-upon goals and operating from the principle that we had all agreed to," recalls Tom. "There were up to eight people on the team and therefore enough different perspectives to determine whether we were on target."

During this exchange, one of the VPs asked Tom a question, which he answered, and the VP returned to the team saying, "Tom feels this way about it." Two other team members called for a time-out, pointing out that the group hadn't agreed to go to O'Brien for his input; furthermore, the VP, he pointed out, had shown disrespect to his team members by going to Tom without them. "When these people confronted their higher-ranking colleagues in this way, it really turned on a light for many in the room," says Tom O'Brien. "The vice president ended up saying, 'You're right. We just broke our circle. We broke your trust . . . One of the principles we began with was that we as a group would come up with specific recommendations, and, as a group, we would work to make sure we were serving broader company needs.' It was a very good learning experience for people who were used to operating in a hierarchical mode."

One of the most significant results of this teamwork is that we have a lot of different people within both companies involved with each other. "We have gone well beyond traditional sales and marketing," explains Tom O'Brien. "And those gains are producing increased sales. More important, we are establishing with our mass-market clients the same kind of personal, value-based relationship as Tom and Kate in the health food trade." We are doing the same thing with four other big accounts: CVS, Target, Hannaford, and Wal-Mart. Each of these companies has its own mission, and some of them overlap nicely with Tom's of Maine's mission—the reason that kicked off our efforts to build such relationships with our retail customers. As a result, we're creating a new model. Before, the buyers' objective was to get the product for the cheapest price; the seller's goal was to sell as much product at the highest price. In our emerging model where the mission is at the center, we're trying to find a common ground, which is usually serving our mutual consumers and their communities around the world. CVS, Target, Hannaford, and Wal-Mart serve a tremendously diverse group of consumers. Each seeks to serve their communities in their own ways. Their annual reports are not exclusively devoted to the bottom line. A good half of Wal-Mart's is focused on building communities.

When Tom O'Brien read Target's annual report he realized that "these guys were into a lot of the same things we are. There were some real overlaps in their mission and ours." He visited five Target retail stores to check to see that what they were saying in their annual reports actually matched what they were doing in their stores. One of the first things he noticed walking through the door was a rack of *Earthsaver* magazines, which Target publishes free for customers. Our sales people didn't know the magazine existed, even though it was part of Target's outreach efforts to help create a sustainable world environment, which, of course, was a fundamental value at Tom's of Maine from day one. When the person at Tom's of Maine called Target about *Earthsaver*, their buyer had no idea Target did anything like this. We eventually learned that Target's community development department was working with a nonprofit foundation to put out the magazine. When we contacted the woman at the foundation who worked with Target and asked her if she did this with other companies, she said that Target had come to them from a mutual acquaintance, and it was the only company they did this with. ''Would you be interested in a partnership with all our accounts to create programs for all their retail customers?'' Tom O'Brien asked. ''Absolutely,'' was her answer. She would provide the editorial content, and Tom's of Maine would provide the customers.

I meet people all the time who think Tom's of Maine is a huge company. They are stunned to find out that we have only eighty-five employees. For a company our size to become such an influential player, we have to be creative. The kinds of new partnerships Tom O'Brien has been forging with these mass-market stores is the definition of creativity. After Tom O'Brien made the deal to create magazines for other customers, one of our managers asked him, ''How is this going to sell more product?'' Such partnerships aren't about selling product; they're about promoting our values in the marketplace and getting others involved. That's our mission—to make money, but to do it while promoting support for the environment and for communities. The better we serve our customers through our mission, the better our sales will be. Our mail from customers bears this out. They know that when they get into business with us, they're buying more than a particular product. They are also promoting values—ours and theirs—to protect the environment.

This is hardly doing business as usual. It's nothing short of a new model, indeed a new *paradigm*, for how all businesses might operate in the next century. We are identifying accounts that share our mission and building partnerships with them. ''Instead of offering to take a certain amount of dollars off the invoice, we can now offer to take fewer dollars off and put them into a partnership built around our shared values,'' explains Tom O'Brien. ''Now Target and Tom's of Maine aren't simply facing off across the table in a sales confrontation with one another. We're sitting on the same side of the table looking for stakeholders in the community or in the nonprofit world who share our values. We're building a new way of commerce which is being shaped by our mission to 'address community concerns, in Maine and around the globe by devoting a portion of our time, talents, and resources to the environment, human needs, arts, and education.' "

INSPIRING CREATIVITY

Over the years, we have picked up some practical ways of encouraging creativity. Simply telling people that they are free to be creative is an amazing start. But your employees must know that you are serious and that they will not be penalized for suggesting new ways of doing things or criticizing the old ways. Most people, however, will have to be convinced that they are capable of being creative, and to that end we have tried various kinds of exercises with our employees to prove to them that though we may not all be artists, we do have imaginations that we can use creatively.

About eight years ago, Kate was eager to break out into new areas of her art, after almost fifteen years of painting watercolors. She eventually discovered new avenues for her art by attending an experimental program at the Charles River Studio Workshop in Watertown, Massachusetts, that helped artists find out more about themselves and their art through play. Presented with a variety of materials, the artists were encouraged to do whatever their creative spirits suggested, to play around with the stuff, focusing not on the end product but on the process of creative play. It was just what Kate needed to jump-start her work into new areas of art. "I needed a setting in which I could play around with possibilities," she says. "Physically playing with things allowed me to try new kinds of art. The key is first to let go of the idea that you have to create something, a product, and instead just pay attention to the process, letting that come from a very deep place, which it will if you allow it. You sit in front of these different materials, man-made and natural—buttons, sticks, stones, fabric, plastic things. You pick what you think you need and build something. Every time you do it, you do something different. It's like looking at where you are in the life of your imagination. Things come out of it. Things become symbols.'' Soon Kate was doing things she had never done before, working in mixed media, experimenting with writing, making paper sculptures and one-of-a-kind books. She even returned to writing poetry.

To help make our own employees more creative, we have experimented with various kinds of workshops. Kate and I have found that many business people are starved for something tangible to do; they need to get their hands dirty. The idea of bringing something tangible into contact with an imagination that has been focused on the analysis of demographic or marketing data, for example, or crunching numbers all day is liberating for many managers. But exploring the creative reaches of their imagination can also be frightening because of the new risks involved. ''But if you focus on play and realize that no one is expecting you to produce a work of art,'' Kate explains, ''the results will be a pleasant surprise. People who never thought about the creative process before suddenly grasp the power and depth of their own imagination. Suddenly they feel the excitement of putting things together without a blueprint or plan.''

Experimenting with a version of Intention #5 last year to encourage the Tom's of Maine staff to venture out, we did a collaborative playing exercise that was fun, revealing, and wild. After an initial reluctance and fear of loosening up, most people find it pretty easy. After all, playing is something that we all did quite naturally when we were children. Kids go into a playroom, pick things up, examine them, play with them, think about how certain items might go together with others, or what might happen if they just dumped a whole box of blocks on the floor. It's amazing how liberated and daring adults feel when they realize they can just make noise or throw things on the floor. We brought in all sorts of materials: feathers, seed pods, sea glass, beads, buttons, streamers, different-colored stones, precious stones, wooden clothespins, film containers, baskets, and a purple scarf. Everyone was asked to pick out three sets of play materials they were drawn to (e.g., stones, clothespins, and spools of thread), sit on the floor, and begin playing. It was fascinating to watch different people work with the different materials, juxtaposing them in different ways, breaking up various orders, trying to put them together in some way that they wanted. Some creations, on first sight, might not seem in any recognizable order, but as you listen to their creators reflect on them, you begin to understand their symbolic meaning, and recognize a unique beauty to each. Such play can be, as Kate says, "a mirror into your imagination."

Once people see what the others are doing, they begin to loosen up. Within the security of the group, people are inclined to step out of their boxes and experiment; they are willing to take more risks. Simply getting out of a chair and down on the floor to work with your hands can be liberating in itself. "This practice of playing can be used to explore a question individually or to problem-solve collectively," explains Kate. "If you don't end up solving your problem immediately, you're at least comfortable because you're doing something with your hands. It's a bit like going on what Buddhists call a 'walking meditation.' There's a mindfulness to it. Playing with things is almost like being in a timeless place, out of that tick-tock clock chronology filled with daily worries and into the more free-floating world of your own dreams or imagination. It's a paradox of being in the moment yet being quite aware. You become expansive in your thinking, which is what you need to solve problems in business. We want people to open up so that they can see new possibilities, which are out there in the collective unconscious if you can stay open."

Each participant was asked to talk about his or her play, and even spend ten minutes "responding" to the results by writing a letter in the "voice" of the play. We divided them up into teams to try playing in a group, consolidating materials from the results of individual playing and creating something new that illustrates or suggests a common ground. There was a path flowing through the middle of some; there were stones and branches, which we interpreted as a sign of nature. In the work of others, there were common signs of motion, of spontaneity, of community, of order. Participants had to answer certain questions: How did they experience taking a risk in individual play and in team play? What skills did they call upon in one kind of play as opposed to the other? How did that relate to venturing out? What contribution did you make? How about your teammates? How did this translate into the interdepartmental teams at Tom's of Maine?

So you see how we went from pure play to tying it into collaborating in teams and then placing that into their actual work experiences at Tom's of Maine. At the end of the morning the participants left with homework—to create and then write about a business or nonbusiness enterprise and create a plan to venture out with it, which they would bring back to the group to discuss. A person's play had an uncanny way of reflecting how their imaginations worked. Most important, seeing the positive results of indulging in play persuades people that business is not all, well, business.

Sometimes letting yourself unwind, permitting your imagination to wander beyond its usual boundaries, or just fooling around can produce real workmanlike benefits. "I think that people have the impression that if you just think harder about something, you will find the answer," says Kate. "Einstein once said, 'Imagination is more important than knowledge.' He used to set up his working space with a place to sit, a place to walk, and a place to stand. I think it's important to have a chance to get out of the way of your usual take on things. When I'm having trouble solving a problem, I have to sit on the floor. Sometimes I just have to take a break from the problem and go outside."

When you're applying your conscious mind with all its intensity to a problem, you're not allowing the other part of your brain to weigh in. Play exercises your nonverbal, spatial, kinesthetic abilities, skills not typically valued in the business world, where verbal personalities, the proverbial "computer brain," and a taste for office politics are favored. But has anyone grown a great business without imagination? And I don't think that anyone can be a great leader without the kind of open imagination and emotional intelligence that allows you to empathize with the people you work with. For some reason, society has relegated such talent to artists and other creative people. But we all have our reserves of creativity, and it makes no sense for business leaders not to mine the imaginative resources that already exist in themselves and their employees. Not everything can be solved in such a linear way. In fact, most things get solved by turning the linear on its head and figuring out a whole new way of looking at the problem. "Seeing something in a whole new light is a kind of metaphor, but it is real, too—it is a new light," says Kate.

Of course, business cannot be all play, and not all ideas are equal. We are finally accountable for what we think and what we do. The values-centered leader, no matter how open and democratic his methods are, no matter how much he encourages his people to be creative and to venture out into new directions, must still hold them accountable. Their work must come up for review.

But in evaluating the work of others, the values-centered leader does things differently. Once again, he or she does it Upside Down, as we will see in the next chapter.

THE ART OF BUSINESS

Traditionally, a "business mind" and a "creative mind" have been seen as polar opposites. The manager analyzes, strategizes, and crunches numbers; the artist dreams, imagines, and creates. Well, entrepreneurs imagine and create, too. And like artists, many managers are in the business of making things (the root meaning, after all, of "manufacturing," which is a combination of the Latin noun for "hand" [manus] and the verb "to make" [facere]. Typically, companies compartmentalize their creativity, hiring their "imagineers" (as the Walt Disney Company calls their visionary types) and letting them do their work in their own department or lab. I believe that most employees are capable of some kind of creativity, if given the opportunity. We all have something of the artist in us. I have learned a lot about creativity from my wife and co-founder Kate, who is an artist and poet. She has also been a prime force in the company's growth and success, somehow managing to be a wife, mother, artist, and businesswoman all at once. I asked Kate to share some of her thoughts about creativity in business:

I think it is very hard to be a creative person in this world, never mind just the business world. Everybody has e-mail, voice mail, and calendars are booked solid. There's no time for simply *being*. The pressure on managers today is so severe that people get very nervous if they aren't being obviously productive. But often the most productive insight of all comes after a period of being fallow. Many scientists will tell you that their most dramatic insights came not in the laboratory or when they were puzzling over an equation at the blackboard, but when they were taking a walk or in a dream. No matter how rational or "scientific" you are, everyone needs that downtime when you are not searching hard for the solution. The imagination needs to come to an opening, to a field, where it feels it can expand. We need to allow ourselves to drift into what I would call "a mind float," when your judgment is suspended and you do not have to give an immediate response. To be creative, we need time to "dwell in possibility," as the poet Emily Dickinson put it.

So for me, the struggle has always been how do I get that time for reflection, contemplation, and solitude in my busy life as both an artist and a businessperson. I've tried various ways of escaping from the day-to-day grind: going off to an island to paint, retreating to an artists' community, even taking a six-month sabbatical from the company to spend two and a half days a week in a monastery in Cambridge, Massachusetts. (Tom arranged his traveling schedule to be at home with our youngest son, who was nine years old at the time.)

Those retreats have made it even clearer to me that what is lacking in the business world is a time for reflection, a time to be discomforted with not having the answer immediately. That is something that all creative people live with. I liken it to that period during childbirth called "transition" when all you want to do is have it over with, when you want to get up and leave. In fact, you are quite angry that you have to do this, to bear this kind of pain. Eventually you work through that and get to a point where you are able to push, and suddenly you feel all that creative energy rushing through you, the birth is happening, and you feel wonderful.

Business people are too focused on results. They want the answer to the problem immediately. But in most creative endeavors, there is that moment when nothing is working. The artist is full of doubt and questions. What is coming out here? What is it going to look like? Is it going to be something that I don't want to have anything to do with? Creativity takes time. The answers are not always obvious, but when we let go of the perfect solution and stay engaged in the process, our intuition finds the way to bring all the threads together. How the imagination works has always been a mystery to me, but it works, as every artist learns.

I guess the challenge for me here at Tom's of Maine is to be creative in a collaborative way because the work that I do as an artist is generally a singular activity. I do think that women have a natural ability to collect people around them and to get people working with them. Women start with the idea of connection, that we are all connected to one another. I read a book recently—*The Female Advantage* by Sally Helgesen (Doubleday, 1990)—that confirmed this for me. Helgesen talks about the ''web of inclusion,'' women leaders seeing themselves not at the top but at the center of a web of connection reaching out to others. She argues that women are particularly tuned in to this early on, so that it is natural for them to pick up the strands of connection and bring people in. I think women leaders get sidetracked when they try to imitate men. That's not to say that women are not focused or purposeful or able to do solitary, singular work. But I believe they already have the flexibility to do collaborative styles of leadership, and it's a shame to overlook that advantage by trying to imitate the way men lead. I have always felt at ease collaborating with others in my business life and have never wanted to do it differently. Maybe I was lucky, because writing and art were my relief from working with other people all day, though now I'm starting to do some collaborative things in my art, too.

In business, I think it is easier to be creative in teams. It is in the group where you begin to get the diversity and the help to get an idea shaped. All those different perspectives do help; they give support to that birthing process. There are so many different elements that come into play with developing a new product. You've got to worry about manufacturing, the ingredients, the chemistry of the ingredients, and how they're going to work together. Marketing is in the back of your mind, as well as costs and other financial factors. The art of it is bringing all these ingredients together, making them into a whole, shaping them into products that are pleasant to use, accomplishing the function that makes this product worth having. What we do here is very much akin to the creative process in the arts, whether the outcome is a new mouthwash, a deodorant, or a toothpaste. They all started with an idea that has gone through a long gestation and that has been formed into something totally unique, totally new. In the end, you can pick up the product, look at it, and say, "I like this creation, and I am going to take it into the world and offer it to other people." That is precisely what you call works of art.

Often people wonder how my experience as a wife, mother, and artist affects my take on business. I tell them about what I call the "three principles of creativity":

1. Be flexible.
2. Be surprised.
3. Be determined.

As a working wife and mother, I have had to do several things at once, and that has increased my appreciation for being flexible. If you wake up one morning and your child is really sick, you've got to be able to decide not to go to work that day or deal with this illness in a way that supports the child. For many years businesses acted as if they'd rather not know that their employees had children. I worked very hard on child care programs and parenting needs at Tom's of Maine. We encourage both mothers and fathers to take time off for a new baby. When you have a child, the bonding experiences for a mother and father are not something that you can postpone or catch up on at a later date. One of the reasons Tom and I live where we do was that our original office was only a block away from the house. I remember going home to nurse my youngest child and then running back to the office.

We have to be creative about coming up with solutions instead of making people pretend they're sick so that they can stay at home to deal with a sick child. We have personal days that people can take;

we have medical and dental insurance that covers children. If you talk to people who work here, many will point out that they wanted to work at Tom's of Maine because of the family-friendly policies and an atmosphere that is supportive of life outside the office. From the start, Tom and I always believed that weekends are a sacred time; evenings are to be with your family or to do personal things so that you can come to work refreshed and ready to work hard all day.

You also have to be prepared to be surprised. Not long ago, we needed a new product to generate short-term cash. We also knew that consumers liked the idea of a baking soda mouthwash. We set out to invent one. The textbooks said that baking soda would break down in an aqueous solution, making it impossible to claim honestly that baking soda still existed in the product. Our scientists assured us that they themselves had seen baking soda turn into sodium carbonate in water. Meantime, our marketing research was telling us that if we could overcome the scientific obstacles to a baking soda mouthwash, lots of people would buy it. We asked our scientists to try it, if only to see how much the baking soda changed. Being flexible, they mixed the baking soda into the mouthwash formula, and *surprise*! The mouthwash somehow kept the baking soda intact.

The bad news was that the baking soda raised the pH enough to make the mouthwash more susceptible to bacterial growth. But we were *determined* to make it work. Accepting the challenge, the chemist in the mouthwash acorn, Libby Dumas, tried boosting the glycerin level in the mouthwash formula, hoping more glycerin, our natural sweetener, would also act as a natural preservative. It did. But an informal taste test of the baking soda mouthwash that Libby did among twenty company employees turned up another surprise: Three out of four tasters preferred the higher-level, glycerin baking soda mouthwash, finding its flavor sweeter and longer-lasting. An unexpected and happy result.

It's how creativity works. You see a possibility, but you can play around with possibilities in your head forever. So you bounce the idea off other people, who are inclined to point out the reasons it won't work. But for a creative person, obstacles become opportunities. If you honor my third principle of creativity, be determined. I tend to take an empirical, hands-on approach to matters. You say it doesn't work? Show me. The textbook said that baking soda would no longer be baking soda in an aqueous solution. But in our mouthwash formula we also had glycerin, which held it together—and made the mouthwash sweeter-tasting in the bargain.

Flexibility, surprise, determination. They can equal creativity, and creativity can make you money. Better still, creativity is a lot of fun.

INTENTION #5 TALKING POINTS

The Four Horsemen of Venturing Out are: To imagine, to dialogue, to create, and to risk.

Imagine the wild ideas that will get you to your goal.

Discuss them with others to build a fuller creative strategy. Creativity is a collaborative process; embrace your employees' creativity, and they will help you venture out.

Create new ways and new systems to be values-centered in achieving your goals. Creativity is not likely to happen unless you encourage it.

Take the risk. Creativity is about reinventing yourself or your business and taking it to a place where no one else has been.

Above all: Be flexible. Be surprised. Be determined.

INTENTION #5 HOMEWORK

We business people tend to be a bit stiff, a little too earnest, and much too committed to rational analysis and number-crunching. To make creative breakthroughs, you have to loosen up. You have to learn to be more playful. So loosen up, pull together some of the materials Kate mentioned in this chapter, invite your Seven Intentions compadre into the room, and get to work (I mean play).

You and your companion should begin by reviewing the "Inspiring Creativity" section of this chapter (p. 137).

Select your materials and keep these ground rules in mind: You have no specific goal in mind; be open to any outcome; there is no right or wrong.

Pick one material, dump it on the floor, then sit down next to it and begin playing with the stuff while you talk about your own experiences of play.

Remember: Be flexible, be surprised, and be determined.

Now choose three materials and begin playing. Add other materials as desired. Allow forty-five minutes to do your play-work silently.

Write a letter to yourself in the voice of the play.

With your buddy, discuss your creation. Your buddy is there to listen, not judge.

Now answer these questions:

- Did you experience any risks in this kind of play?
- What skills did you call upon?
- How does this relate to venturing out?
- How did this play session reflect the workings of your imagination?

Take a break. When you return, write a plan to realize your vision, and then discuss it with your playmate.

8

Assess

INTENTION #6
No matter how creative we might choose to be or how unique we are in the marketplace, we are still accountable to our values, visions, and goals. Managing Upside Down is a trial-and-error process, and assessment requires constant affirmation and editing.

In one of my regular meetings with my COO, Tom O'Brien, early in the fall of 1998, he informed me that our customers were having trouble finding Tom's of Maine products on their supermarket and drugstore shelves. He had suspected as much since he arrived at the company, and now both consumer mail and sales were confirming his suspicion. He then proceeded to speak passionately about the need to focus on our brand identity in our packaging. In order for our products to be more easily identifiable on the shelf, he argued, we had to make our logo more consistent from package to package.

This criticism was a quandary for me, frankly. I liked our packaging. Our logo had been around for eighteen years, and Kate and I played a central role in creating it. Furthermore, I'm not someone interested in homogeneity for the sake of homogeneity. In fact, one of the greatest strengths of Tom's of Maine is its *heterogeneity*. Success had come our way because we were different. We were the first to sell a natural toothpaste. We had a complex set of values, and no company trumpeted the benefits of diversity more than Tom's of Maine. I was not inclined to change my packaging simply because one product's packaging was not a carbon copy of another's.

But I gave Tom's critique of our packaging some thought and finally said to myself, "Hey, come on! This is why you asked this guy to join the company"—for his ideas, his experiences, his expertise, his advice, and his criticism. It also occurred to me that the Johnson & Johnson logo appeared on bandages, baby products, contact lens packages, and every other thing Johnson & Johnson made. I realized this was the kind of brand identity Tom was talking about. I also realized that he was right, particularly at a time when we were about to introduce a whole new line of herbal products. We needed something that we could put on all our products that said, "Even though you've never seen these items before, they come from the same company you have already come to trust."

Every business leader has to be held accountable. A values-centered manager, however, has to be open to an even broader assessment. I would be a charlatan if I pontificated about reimagining American commerce and didn't hold myself—and my company—accountable to the values and goals I have set. The values-centered leader needs timely feedback measured against strategic business plans, the mission, and the company's destiny. Upside Down Managers have three main obligations: (1) serving our customers; (2) performing that service in a way that doesn't harm people, the community, or the environment; and (3) making money.

That's a new way of looking at the world. We are breaking new ground. At this stage, Managing Upside Down is a trial-and-error process, which is all the more reason we values-centered leaders have to be more open to editing and constructive criticism.

THE BENEFITS OF A FRESH EYE

So when Tom O'Brien raised the logo issue, I bridled for a moment, gave it some thought, realized he had a point, and went to work researching the issue. Within twenty-four hours of our meeting, I decided to put together a team to come up with a solution to our identity problem. And since were dealing with the company logo, a symbol that evokes emotion from our customers as well as those of us who've been with the company for a long time, I preferred that this team be a small group of people with a lot of experience in the company. I wanted Kate to be a member; she has an intuitive feel for design and decades of experience with our packaging decisions. I included our graphics designer, Rod Williams, with whom Kate and I have worked for twenty-five years. I also brought in the head of our brands group, Melissa Skelton, and, of course, Tom O'Brien. I chose to take the lead in this initiative myself.

Immediately, I headed off to the local markets and bought $300 worth of products of brands I thought presented a clear identity of what they were and those that seemed muddled. I also created a list of aims that the team ought to consider beyond Tom O'Brien's concern that the look of the logo be consistent from package to package. I wanted the logo to have "personality," a certain kind of particularity that squared with our complex values but also gave the appropriate emotional charge. While I wanted the packaging to be identifiable as a Tom's of Maine product, I also wanted each product to have its own singular package. Our mission vows that we will be "distinctive in our products." Overall, I wanted the design to be clean, simple, humble, and honest. With all these considerations in mind, the team went off to work on some sample designs.

We then took the design team's sample logos to consumers. Their response: loyal Tom's of Mainers all, they did not want us to stray too far from the original logo. But they were interested in the choice of the color green for the logo, which would give our packaging a consistent look from product to product—just as Tom O'Brien had advocated. A logo that stood out in the same way on every package seemed to provide the customer with a sense of familiarity and trust. They already liked our products, and for them the Tom's of Maine logo meant, "This is a product that will work for you." We will be using the new logo design for all our new products, and we eventually will change the packaging on all our old products so that all our products will have the same logo design. Tom O'Brien's candid assessment of the logo has also turned out to be wise. And though I flinched at first, we took his critique seriously and finally agreed. Afterward, Tom told me that he felt very much affirmed by my support and by the process.

Tom O'Brien's fresh eye has helped us all to be more accountable to the mission. As soon as he arrived, he quickly noted some inconsistencies between what we preached and what we practiced. He assessed the company's commitment to the outsert program and found it wanting. As I wrote in Chapter 2, when he found people still concerned about the expense of including outserts on the deodorant packaging, he informed them that including information about the company with the product could not be compromised, not even for budgetary reasons, especially for budgetary reasons. Similarly, when he was told that inserts for our bar soap would get moldy and outserts would be too expensive, he called a meeting of the marketing and sales people. "What is it that you don't get?" he asked. "Isn't the mission clear?" He wondered out loud if we would send a product out without fragrance. Of course not, everyone agreed. He then pointed out that our informational inserts and outserts were as essential to a Tom's of Maine product as its natural ingredients and fragrance. Informing and educating our customers, he pointed out, is also part of who we are. Tom's of Maine is promoting not just personal hygiene but also social responsibility and environmental sustainability.

I thought that I had discouraged internal politicking and turf battles between departments by letting a few of those department heads go. But soon after Tom's arrival, he informed me that he had never witnessed so much infighting, not even at Procter & Gamble, which has over 103,000 employees worldwide to our eighty-five. People were just too protective of their departments. After some thought, we decided on a drastic measure: to wipe out departments altogether.

FLATTENING THE HIERARCHY

I had been encouraging more interdependence and collaboration between departments for almost five years. I called it "flattening the hierarchy." But my managers were mystified as to how to pull it off; they were unable to break away from the old budget-centered behavior. I kept talking about the mission, but not everyone could internalize it. It wore me down, and Kate and I began exploring selling the company.

Once we decided not to sell and found a COO/partner for me, we were still faced with the problem of how to transform the culture of the company into one that was as values-centered as its owners. The resistance to living the mission persisted among my executives. But soon Tom O'Brien began to out-Tom Tom Chappell. Even I was amazed. Tom took my concession that the managers had "worn me down" as evidence that the company's mission was nowhere near as centered as I had believed (see box on p. 165). Tom said he was convinced that we had "a great set of values," but that though Kate and I, along with a few other top executives, were genuinely values-centered, the rest of the organization was not quite there. It would be his job, he said, to get the company centered around the mission by hiring people more in tune with our values and promoting people who were comfortable with collaboration. The control freaks would have to go.

We decided, in fact, to turn the whole place upside down. The company's organizational structure would be called an "organizational system." We wanted to see the organization not as the typical power pyramid but as a series of interlocking and interdependent circles connected by the same common vision based on the same values. The company's goals would be everyone's goals. Three years later, there is virtually no remnant of the old departments at Tom's of Maine. Marketing and sales have been folded into teams for Brand Development, Consumer Research, and Customer Business Development, an effort to deal more directly with the stores we sell to. The manufacturing end of the company, including the plant and purchasing the ingredients for our products, now comes under Products Supply. Each of these teams is headed up by a group team leader who is an officer of the company. I'm the group team leader of New Product Development, which includes the crucial subteam of Research and Development and the new product acorns.

The new acorn system itself has stifled the internal politicking, while giving members of the product development teams and other initiative groups (the kiosks team and the group researching the logo, for example) autonomy, a sense of owning the issues they're involved in, and an opportunity to use their gifts and skills. More important, the acorns reinvigorated our product development exponentially. Stymied for thirty-six months without a new product, within a year after the acorn system had been kicked off, we created twenty-five new oral and body care products and seventy-five new items in the wellness category.

Yet even such an unqualified success as the acorn system benefited from assessment. One of the original champions I appointed did not work out. Although she had the creativity and business experience that seemed perfect for the job, she was unable to counter the negativity from various departments that had been stalling our R&D for more than a year, the very thing the acorn system had been invented for. I had to replace her as a champion.

We eventually edited the acorn system even further. A few of the new acorns were still short their marketing person, and I asked Tom O'Brien to make the appointments. He advised against it, explaining that he didn't think our marketing people were creative enough. "They are going to be a barrier to you," he said, warning that they were too eager to point to what was wrong about an idea rather than what might be possible. I decided to limit those acorns to their champions and scientists and get feedback from customers via the new consumer research team we were setting up. This has turned out to be more interactive than anything we've ever had: Consumer Research bounces a product idea off a group of consumers, turning the results over to the acorn scientist whose job it was to create the actual product. With a product prototype in hand, we can then go back to consumers for their reaction. Most important, we had sidestepped the negativity of the previous product development process. Our new ideas were now in the hands of a small group of people who wanted the idea to work because it was either their idea or they had nurtured it from infancy. Assessing whether it did work was up to someone else.

The whole look of our company now matches its values. We are committed to a partnership model of doing business. The company's power has been spread throughout the organization by giving each person a specific role to play. Their key relationships also have been specified. These are now the standards of who supervises whom and how people are evaluated annually. Empowerment really does work, but only, we have found, when you get the hierarchy out of the way. In the traditional hierarchical organization, the value of an employee is based on his or her place in the pecking order and length of service. Employees are viewed only partially, without much regard for their real talents and potential for contributing to the success of the company. Nothing could be more demeaning or put a bigger damper on motivation.

ACCOUNTABILITY REQUIRES MORE THAN A CALCULATOR

When a company is accountable only to the bottom line, all it takes is an accountant to check on how you're doing. Tom's of Maine, however, has set a mission ''to provide meaningful work, fair compensation, and a safe, healthy work environment that encourages openness, creativity, self-discipline, and growth.'' The best way to achieve those goals is through a collaborative way of doing business, and to that end, we have launched a training program, using a version of the Seven Intentions, to help our employees work better together, particularly in groups.

In the past, meetings were typically dominated by one voice. No one else's opinion was even solicited. Anyone with an idea who was naturally shy or insecure was bound to be bulldozed by the big personalities in the room. And when people spoke up, it was usually to torpedo an idea rather than bolster it. Working with outside facilitators, we have been training our managers to be facilitators themselves. Everyone takes a turn running a meeting, and those who show a talent for facilitating meetings are encouraged to develop that skill. We have worked hard on creativity and giving the kind of structure to group meetings that encourages people to speak their minds and trains them in how to contribute constructively to a meeting. In the old days, employees would complain, "They never ask for my opinion." Now, it is part of everyone's job to speak up. We provide big pads of newsprint propped on an easel at each meeting where people are encouraged to write what they think, and then it gets discussed. When we were planning the launch of our new baking soda mouthwash, the acorn champion, in this case Kate, came up with a marketing campaign that she presented to the Campaign Team, a committee set up to help acorn champions launch new products into the marketplace. Members of the committee stepped right up to the newsprint and offered their opinions about Kate's strategy, what they liked, and what their concerns were. As a result, we have gained access to the minds and thoughts, not to mention the knowledge and the wisdom, of our employees.

We have transformed the level of participation in meetings. All it took was providing a structure for allowing people to speak their minds, which, in turn, releases the creativity that was always there. It has been incredible. Our ultimate goal is for everyone to understand that in a values-centered company, everything that we do must be accountable not to the boss but to the company's values. In the long term, personalities in every company are bound to change at every level. Even the Chappells who control the company will come and go. And if the Chappells don't survive as controlling owners over the next fifty to one hundred years, the core values of Tom's of Maine will. No one person will make the company what it is. Tom's of Maine will be its values.

To assure that this will happen, we have turned the structure of our company upside down.

OUR BIGGEST ASSESSMENT YET—RESTRUCTURE THE COMPANY!

Is there any phrase in American business more terrifying than "employee review"? If you want your people to be your biggest creative resource, you have to let them know they are allowed to make mistakes. This doesn't happen when the big boss sits behind his desk and lambastes his subordinates for not measuring up to some middle manager's version of a job well done. Personnel evaluations are unavoidable, but they do not have to be so judgmental and subjective. Personalities differ; people have different strengths (and weaknesses) and work at different speeds. In revamping our own employee evaluations, we have tried to get away from a system where one boss gets the final word.

Now that Tom's of Maine is divided into interlocking groups of teams, each employee on those teams has a specific role description that is very clear on what his or her job is. What employees are accountable for is also spelled out in detail in a "work development plan." By substituting teams for a departmental pecking order, we have set up a more open, collegial system of feedback where various key members of teams offer opinions on how others are pursuing the company's goals in their particular roles. We have stripped the subjectivity out of the evaluation process by providing employees with a set of expectations that is clearly articulated in our role descriptions and work development plans. We all have to see ourselves as agents of the mission with clear roles and responsibilities.

My role in this new system is to help the company discern what its beliefs, mission, and reason for being are. I have to look ahead and help articulate the company's goals. It's also my job to bring resources into the company, the right financing, the right people. It's up to me to motivate those people. (Of course, the beauty of being a private company is that I also get to pick who they are.) Then there's my partnership with my COO, which has turned out to be collaborative and collegial. But once we have agreed on what direction we're going in and what the strategy is, it's also my job to assess where we are.

Protecting turf or satisfying a boss should not register in our assessment process. Neither builds toward the destiny of the organization. We try to link our evaluations of employees to the key indicators of the company's success: the performance of our products and our commitment to the community and the environment, while making a fair financial return. Assessment thus becomes a kind of R&D process that checks on the health of the organization and its mission, informing us if we have gotten closer to achieving our objectives.

IT'S NOT US AGAINST THEM

The values-centered organization is *team-built*. Too often CEOs and other corporate leaders believe that they have to be perfect. The Upside Down approach assumes at the start that we are all imperfect. No one person has the time to do everything; no one can be a wizard at every skill. Unfortunately, too many people in positions of authority in the business world are inclined to hire yes-men, people who will rubber-stamp their policies. Others hire executives who are supposed to be perfect at marketing or sales or science, and when these hires disappoint the big boss, he hauls them into his office and criticizes them for not being perfect, which, of course, they never could be in the first place. Such negative, judgmental evaluations are demeaning and, above all, unfair.

The Upside Down approach is to say that every business is a community that needs a full complement of gifts. If someone is not good at something that you need, then add someone else to the team. That is what a leader must do. The head of my R&D is a pharmacognosist. I made the decision to have the science of pharmacognosy leading the company and not chemistry. A recent assessment of R&D revealed that we needed a top-notch formulations chemist who also knows pharmaceuticals to direct our staff chemists. I couldn't very well criticize my head of research for not filling that role because from the outset I knew that chemistry was not her specialty. Instead, she and I assessed the situation. We reviewed where we were going and what we needed to get there. We also got a look at a standard of what was possible from a pharmaceutics expert we had hired as a consultant. We looked at what we were up against not as opponents, but as a team.

Assessment must be an open and honest process and not an inquisition. The company has moved far away from the boss–subordinate relationship. Those in leadership roles are playing more supervisory and coaching roles with the people in their groups. Once employees know what is expected, once they understand what skills it takes to get the job done and that there are people around the company who will help them improve those skills, they become very motivated. We have been working hard to find the best ways to evaluate ourselves, to focus on our gifts and strengths, and to improve in the areas where we need work. The leader of our Consumer and Brand Development Group, Melissa Skelton, knew from her own experience in other organizations how important assessing performance was, but she knew she could not use the kind of employee evaluation system she knew from her days at Procter & Gamble. She decided to experiment with some ideas she had that would tap into what she found unique about Tom's of Maine, namely our mission's commitment to encourage creativity, openness, and growth, to seek a diversity of gifts, and to foster teamwork. This "reflection and goal-setting process," as Melissa calls it, has been such a success among the employees in her Consumer and Brand Development Group that we are trying it out in other areas of the company. But once again, the guiding light was the mission. It was the mission that told Melissa what she had to focus on in coming up with an assessment process for Tom's of Maine, just as it is the mission that guides each employee in his or her job (see box on p. 169).

But who are the trustees for the mission? The board of directors are, at least in the case of Tom's of Maine. They and the owners have established the values that they believe in strongly enough to commit the entire company to. In turn, they delegate their authority to the officers of the company. Assessment is the way in which those with authority hold those with power accountable for moving the organization toward its destiny. But the guiding spirit of this kind of assessment is the goal of improving the organization. Assessment can never be just about discipline.

In fact, managing by values is so new that negativity is really out of place. When you break the mold or come up with an entirely new paradigm, you will have to move forward in a context of uncertainty. People are unlikely to risk failure if someone is standing over them with a stick. We must nurture risk-takers and be generous with our praise. Managers are inclined to jump on their subordinates when they make mistakes, while treating a job well done as what people are being paid to do. Great leaders know that nothing can motivate workers like a pat on the back. Now. Don't save your encouragement for three months from now, when success is assured. Employees need to hear, "I really like what you have just done." Who will take a risk if he or she never has heard a leader say, "Tell me more about your new idea"?

EVEN CEOS NEED AFFIRMATION

When Tom O'Brien joined the company, we both were aware that we were entering a risky relationship. I was giving up a lot, and he was taking on a lot. We have built our partnership on two things: (1) The company had done its homework, creating a mission that has been in place for almost a decade representing not only what we thought the company was but what we wanted it to be, always; and (2) Tom O'Brien and I trusted one another's integrity. This trust helped us turn the risky give-and-take part of our relationship into its foundation. Our partnership is about taking advantage of each other's gifts. I am not afraid to concede to him that I'm a lousy manager, because one of the reasons I hired him is that translating a strategy to large groups of people is his strong suit. He is terrific at writing long memos that weave the company's values into our objectives and how we plan to achieve them. I am not afraid to congratulate him on his work. And he is not shy about telling me how much he has learned from me.

Criticism is important. But praise is nice, too. And when criticism is tempered with praise, it is a lot easier to stomach. It also helps to admit you were wrong. My immediate reaction to Tom O'Brien's insistence that we needed to focus more on our brand identity and our logo was that he was wrong. But after some thought I realized he was right, and told him so.

My decision to put a pharmacognosist instead of a chemist in charge of R&D was unpopular within the company. As I was working on this chapter, Tom O'Brien came in to report about a meeting he and a team of five of our people, including the head of R&D, had with 120 people from store management in the Wild Oats organization. The Wild Oats people, according to Tom, were stunned to learn that a pharmacognosist was head of R&D at Tom's of Maine. They couldn't ask her enough questions. Tom also told me that some of my chief critics on the chemist-pharmacognosist issue had admitted to him that I evidently knew what I was doing when I put a pharmacognosist in charge. They had made this concession not because they wanted to suck up to the boss, but because they had come to realize my decision was turning out to be good for the company.

HOW TO CENTER VALUES IN YOUR COMPANY—THE SEVEN INTENTIONS

The Seven Intentions are tools for change. This book is both a manifesto for a new way of doing business—the values-centered way—and a tool kit for how to learn how to do it, how to become skilled at Managing Upside Down. Warning: You never graduate from the

Seven Intentions. You only make progress. Consider yourself a pioneer.

The Seven Intentions, too, are a work in progress. I tried these ideas out first with the Boulder Business Group, a dozen CEOs, entrepreneurs, and executive vice presidents of companies with annual sales ranging from one million to over a billion dollars with at least one thing in common: They wanted to know how to manage by values, particularly in the face of the obstacles created by venture capitalists, large customers, and their own natural pride and self-interest. Sound familiar?

Like you, their intuitions and their strong values made them think there had to be a better way. These were people who said they believed in a clean environment, who wanted to be decent human beings. People in their companies had great new ideas that got swept aside as soon as business slowed or there were budget cuts. Another common complaint: The venture capitalists on my board aren't the least bit interested in hearing what they call ''these fuzzy-feely notions.'' They want performance and results. The entrepreneurs in the group reported that as soon as they brought in venture capitalists, they lost control of their businesses and eventually had to sell out and exit.

Sound familiar? These business people were looking for new ways to motivate people, to reward them. They wanted to get values into the marketplace. But they didn't have a clue about how to do it.

They were intrigued by the story of Tom's of Maine told in my first book, *The Soul of a Business*, and wanted to talk about the issues it raised. I created a safe circle for them to share their frustrations and different perspectives once a month with the same people. I wanted them to have some tools to move beyond their frustrations to provide the kind of leadership that could integrate values into their workplaces. To that end, they agreed to take a crack at a preliminary version of the Seven Intentions, and the version that you are reading owes the Boulder Business Group a great debt.

I offered them a way, my way, with the proviso that I did not have all the answers. Values-centered leadership was a relatively new idea that struck at the heart of American business. All I could do was offer what I had learned from my struggle to make my values drive my company, still very much a work in progress. They volunteered to be the pilot project for my effort to create a way to train other managers in Managing Upside Down.

ASSESSING THE SEVEN INTENTIONS

After getting together regularly for about eight months, getting to know each other and sharing our business experiences, and working through my steps toward values-centered leadership, the group met on Intention #6 and assessed its experience of going through the Seven Intentions. "I no longer feel like I'm alone," said one member. "This group validates and supports things I truly believe in at a deeper level." Many pointed to the challenge that the group had posed to them to be as open about values on the job as they were in the group. "What I like about the Seven Intentions," said another member, "is that it provides some real structure and some specific steps for doing the work. It is a course to follow. It is not just coming to share our frustrations. It points us in a proactive posture to actually be able to make progress."

And progress sometimes means looking for another job. During this assessment, one group member announced that he was leaving his position as a senior financial officer and partner because he was frustrated that the company was not oriented enough toward values; he had become frustrated with the direction in which the company was going. Being part of the group had helped him realize that he had become so divided about what his company was up to that the only way he could salvage his own integrity, he decided, was to leave. He had no idea what he would do next, but he was smiling again. He thanked the group for providing him with the strength and courage to make this decision.

Some members were concerned about whether the Seven Intentions was a closed or open system. Were we making a commitment to each other as a group, or a commitment to ourselves? I pointed out that it is difficult to separate the two. The first priority is yourself. You will not be able to change anybody else until you first change yourself. In that sense, a process like the Seven Intentions is a selfish enterprise. Yet by changing yourself you will find that you have become dependent on the group, with a sense of responsibility to its members.

The Boulder Business Group proved to me that there is a hunger among executives to talk about their desire to get values into the workplace and unload the frustrations that are bound to go along with that task. People are looking for solutions. They want a new, more caring paradigm for American enterprise.

ASSESSING THE SEVEN INTENTIONS AT TOM'S OF MAINE

After the Boulder experience, I continued to think about the Seven Intentions, refining them as a training tool for doing business the values-centered way. I also wanted this program to help not just CEOs and entrepreneurs but all employees, from middle managers right down to administrative assistants. I have learned that if you wanted to build a values-centered company, then you had better have everyone in the building on board. In 1998, I put together a group of fifteen people in Kennebunk, ten from Tom's of Maine and the rest business people from the community, and with the help of outside facilitators took them through the Seven Intentions. By the time you read this, all my managers and most of my employees will have participated in a program on the Seven Intentions.

It has transformed the place. We have changed the culture of Tom's of Maine from the traditional fear-driven domain where politics and turf battles got in the way to a team-based, values-centered, honest, and mutually caring community. People have not only opened up (to themselves as well as to each other), they have become more focused on the work at hand. We have found that the Seven Intentions have given us the permission to be yourself and express yourself. There is a greater sense of community—and the deep trust that comes with the feeling of being connected by common values and pursuing the same goals. The result has been a strong commitment to the work and objectives of the company.

At the center of this transformation in the company's values is the mission. But the mission did not make it happen. The Seven Intentions have changed Tom's of Maine by making the mission become more alive. In 1989, we had written down what we as a company believed in and what we valued. A decade later, the Seven Intentions have helped us turn those words into a genuinely values-centered company. The results have been absolutely incredible.

But the Seven Intentions is a trial-and-error process. Integrating values into a company is a new thing, and we can all learn from each other. That is one of the reasons I have tried to be so candid about our experiences at Tom's of Maine, both good and bad. As we all continue our experiment, you, too, will have to tell us what works.

That itself is a breakthrough. Traditionally, when a company discovers its secret to success, it is loath to broadcast it. Why should Coca-Cola tell everyone else how to create the most lucrative taste in history? Did Macy's talk to Gimbel's? But when your goal in business is more than profit, indeed, when your goal is to change the way business is done, you cannot keep any secrets.

You have to *pass it on*. And that brings us to the next and final Intention.

"FROM THE DESK OF THE COO"

We are usually not our own best judges. Throughout this book, I have offered several examples of our struggle at Tom's of Maine to live up to our values. Frankly, I thought it would be easier. But doing business in an entirely new, upside down way is bound to run into obstacles. You've read my assessment in this chapter. I've also reported on how Tom O'Brien has put our feet to the fire and pressed us to live up to the mission. Here's his frank assessment of what a values-centered leader is up against and how Tom's of Maine is doing:

We all have choices to make, and we have to take responsibility for them. At Tom's of Maine, the first choice that every employee has to make, as an individual, is to embrace the company's beliefs. Can you do that? If you agree, then you have an obligation to operate from this orientation. That becomes the standard of accountability.

We often run into trouble around here when we go outside the company for something, a recyclable package, for instance. One of our purchasing people confers with someone from a packaging company who says we cannot give you a recycled package. After trying ten times to find a recyclable package, our person will come back with a package. I'll ask if it's recyclable, and the answer is, "No, there is no such thing as a recyclable package for this product." For the past year, for instance, we've been trying to get a recyclable deodorant package. We have been selling a natural deodorant, but our package isn't recyclable. People are starting to say that there is no recyclable package in the market, so we shouldn't worry so much about it. You start to accept what others say. They wear you down. And then you begin compromising on other issues. Yes, it's plastic (and therefore not recyclable), but not that plastic. We rationalize it: "Hey—we're giving them a natural product, which is better than what's out there. So what if it has a little plastic in the packaging?"

Instead, we should be asking if we have another choice. Should we even be in business in that category if it means compromising our basic values? Someone might argue that we could not build the company without that product. Bull! Our mission calls for us to have recyclable packaging. We can't just throw out that fundamental value to accept the status quo for one product.

In my opinion, the quickest way to hurt the company is to compromise its mission. If you have a loyal consumer who has bought into the Tom's of Maine proposition that he's been sold a recyclable product and that he really likes the fact that your company is promoting environmental sustainability, when he finds out that your package is not recyclable, you're in big trouble. Not only do you turn customers off from buying Tom's of Maine products, but you can also turn them into skeptical consumers who probably won't support any company that is environmentally responsible, or who will at least think twice before doing so. You do more damage than good.

We have a statement of beliefs and a mission, which represent the deepest beliefs of Tom and Kate. First and foremost, it is their mission. Fine. The challenge is, how do you get the entire organization enrolled in those beliefs and that mission? How do you get them to buy into it? How do you reinforce it day to day? The goal is to make those values part of who they are. We can say we are a values-centered organization, but if we are not making decisions day in and day out using those values consciously, we end up going in directions we do not want to go. You just can't assume that because your values are written down that you are a values-driven company. It is not about hanging your values on the wall or talking about them. People need to be able to see the results of operating on those values. The values, too, need to be reassessed and edited, because an organization that is truly learning about itself should want to build on its beliefs and make them clearer. We can also point to the areas where we are really doing a good job and the places where we are falling short . . .

You put your values at the center of your company by operating according to those values day in and day out throughout your organizational structure. Centering your values starts with the recruiting and hiring process. But how you make your decisions is bound to have the biggest impact on your organizational culture. No other activity in a company takes up more time and energy than decision-making. Those decisions have to reflect the mission. The values are primary. It isn't even a balance. You can't hedge and ask before making every decision, "Can we build a business and do it according to these values?" We *are* those values, and if we execute our plans in a way that is consistent with those beliefs and mission, the results will come.

Sure, you are inclined to fall into a balancing act because the world around you starts pulling you off-center, away from your values. But think about a company as if it were a human being. Human beings all have the potential to be centered. We all have a soul. We have a sense of self. For some it's stronger than for others. I can assure you that people who have a stronger sense of self are more consistent in their lives and have more enduring friendships and relationships. Typically, they are productive people with low transaction costs.

An organization is exactly the same way. It is just a collection of those types of individuals. Orientation is very, very important for any company that wants to operate first and foremost from a belief center with those beliefs driving top-line growth and bottom-line profit. And that is really challenging, particularly as we grow the company and hire new people, diluting the community here with people who might not have the same values orientation. That tends to create a dysfunctional sense of balancing and compromising, and a struggle around how we operate the business.

But it doesn't have to be about compromise. If we come to the conclusion that we cannot come up with recyclable packaging for our deodorant, then maybe we should not be in the deodorant business. Our reason for being—solving consumer needs with science, plants, and minerals—is pretty broad. We can be in all sorts of categories.

Accountability is often harder in an entrepreneurial-founders' organization. It's not like working at a place like Procter & Gamble or some other big company where if you can't build capacity and commitment to the company's goals, then you will not be successful. If you don't do it their way, you will not get ahead. When Tom Chappell admits that his managers "wore him down" into compromising on the outsert/insert program and on the recyclable problem with the deodorant packaging, that is extremely revealing: It means that he was operating in one way, and they were operating differently. When I came in, many people around here expected me to be more like them. That revealed to me that Tom's values, the company's values, had not yet been wholly institutionalized. That is why many entrepreneurial-founders' companies reach a plateau. The minute the founder steps away from the business, the thing tends to spin out of control and sales decrease. It is because the founders never institutionalized or centered the organization on their fundamental beliefs. They hired people used to operating from a totally different vantage point and never gave them the tools to convert.

What we are now trying to do at Tom's of Maine is to work out the tools to convert people to doing business according not just to values, but to *our* values, our mission. You can create incredible momentum in organizational capacity by institutionalizing your beliefs and mission and getting them centered into the everyday decision-making of the organization. What is happening now is that people are actually starting to challenge one another in meetings without Tom Chappell around. It doesn't matter if Tom is around, this is what we believe in, this is what we signed on for. This is what we are being held accountable for.

It is a slow process. It is a difficult process. We are a values-focused company, but even Tom's of Maine is not yet a wholly values-centered organization. But we are working at it every day and making some wonderful progress.

ASSESSING PERFORMANCE THE TOM'S OF MAINE WAY

I agree with Tom O'Brien: it is a slow and difficult process becoming a truly values-centered organization. To speed it up, we needed a better way to assess our employees, and our head of Consumer and Brand Development, Melissa Skelton, "fooled around with some ideas," as she puts it, and came up with a way of keeping up with how our employees are doing. A P&G alumna who also happens to be an ordained Episcopalian priest, Melissa has always been very interested in the connection between, as she puts it, "freeing people to become better human beings and making things happen organizationally." It's her gift, and Tom's of Maine is blessed to have someone like Melissa showing us all how we can use our unique gifts to benefit the Tom's of Maine community. Her achievement is a good example of how a values-centered leader can spread the word throughout a company. But let Melissa tell you about it:

Tom's of Maine is not your usual company. But even a unique place like this needs a way of assessing the performance of its employees and setting goals for the future. We really did not have a corporate way to do such assessments. From my experience in other organizations, I knew about the power and the health of having an assessment and goal-setting process that really works. In every company, people have a job to do, but too often they forget why they're doing it. If each of us does his or her job right, the company will achieve its goals. A company-wide assessment process helps people get connected to the larger goals of the company. With those goals clearly in mind, people aren't wasting their time doing things that are not important to the grand scheme of things.

I also had another aim. I wanted to show how liberating it could be to step back from the daily demands of work and see what we've done. And better still, to get credit for our achievements. We would also lay out the goals of the future and focus on them. But the real challenge was how to recast the traditional corporate assessment for Tom's of Maine, to tap into what was uniquely Tom's, namely, that spirit to honor the individual's need to generate new ideas and the company's commitment to getting its people to explore their own gifts and figure out how such talents might benefit both themselves and Tom's of Maine.

I have always been very interested in the connection between human development and productivity. Building on people's strengths, seeing what they need to work on, supporting specific behaviors, that's an awesome process for me. I am an extrovert who likes to sit with people and explore their gifts. I also love coaching, especially the creativity of working with others. I guess it's the priest in me who just likes helping people find out what they're good at. So I set out to see if I could come up with some kind of assessment process that would work for Tom's.

For me, one of the most exciting things was to create a language of assessment without actually using the word "assessment," which for most people conjures up negative feelings. I wanted people to view our assessment process at Tom's as taking time out to think about their job and how they fit into the goals of the company. I decided to call it, perhaps somewhat awkwardly but at least descriptively, a "reflection and goal-setting process." I asked the nine people on my team over a six-week period to go through the following steps:

1. Reflect on your past accomplishments, what gifts you have, and what gifts and skills you might need to strengthen or develop.

To make sure they gave themselves time to think about these things, I asked people to schedule time for reflection, to book it on their calendars.

2. Pick five or six people in the company to engage in a dialogue about your gifts and the areas you might need to develop or work harder on.

I emphasized that they should ask a lot of questions about how these people saw them, how they viewed what they did, and what they offered to the life at Tom's of Maine. I told them to listen carefully, even to use a tape recorder, and then go back with more questions, thinking hard about what they heard. "What gifts or skills would you like to see me develop?" was not the kind of question that anyone had asked fellow workers before. More important, this information was not being fed to anyone's boss or manager. The answers to the questions were for the employee who asked them to think about. As a result, their co-workers were inclined to be a lot more candid.

3. Schedule time with yourself (again, book it on your calendar) and draft (a) a list of your preliminary goals related to the company's mission/beliefs/reason for being statements along with the priorities of your group; and (b) a list of your own ideas for the things you need to do to take advantage of your gifts or skills and to work on the areas within yourself you want to develop.
4. Check in with the Consumer and Brand Development Group on how the process is going for everyone.
5. Meet with the person you work most directly with, share what you've written, and gather his or her ideas.

This was the first time anyone had met with the person they worked most directly with. I proposed that these meetings last for forty-five minutes. In a few cases, "the person they worked most directly with" was me. The manager's task in this kind of assessment is to help refine the process and point to the common denominators arising from the different conversations.

6. Revise what you've written to reflect the conversation you had with the person you work most directly with. This is about working on your existing strengths, strengthening and developing gifts and skills, and developing business-related goals for the future.

The result was a list of accomplishments, goals, and skills and gifts to develop. The employees then discussed these final writeups with me and the other manager, solidifying what their goals were and the areas they needed to develop—as a person working in this particular company, Tom's of Maine.

It was great. We had turned the traditional personnel assessment process upside down. Instead of an employee visiting the boss's office to hear what management thought of his or her work, the employee had compiled a list of pluses and minuses and was seeking a manager's opinion on how to proceed. Instead of a top-down approach, my job was to build on their own (and their colleagues') assessments of how they were doing.

And progress was made. For example: While everyone had to learn how to facilitate meetings, it was clear that a few people had developed into expert team facilitators. I told them I wanted them to get even better, to be able to handle a meeting no matter how complex it might be. One person volunteered that she needed to become more assertive. I agreed, and advised that not being so was holding her back.

And so it went. Each person worked with a manager to refine and focus the information that he or she had collected and to hammer out goals for the future. We agreed on the amount of money and time training would take, and the manager coached them on various ways they might achieve those goals. The message was: "You need to manage your own assessment process." No one was preparing a document that would be reviewed and then filed away. This was about how everyone might be able to make their skills and gifts work better for them and for Tom's of Maine.

Meantime, I realized that we as a company were unclear about what skills we valued. I knew from my own experience in business what skills were necessary to succeed (e.g., leadership and the ability to analyze data), but as a relative newcomer to Tom's, I was curious about what skills my colleagues thought were essential for this company. I met with people around the company and asked them to answer the question, "When work is going well and I'm feeling good about my job, what are the skills that I notice?" One area that kept coming up was communication, not just getting you message across to someone else but a dialogue, full and honest. Another skill that Tom's of Maine employees valued was the ability to plan and organize in a disciplined way so as to get things done.

Surprisingly, there was not much talk about analysis or even creativity. I think most people had been relying on the founders to provide that. And sure enough, when I questioned Tom and Kate about what skills they thought were most important for the success of the company, they put creativity at the top of the list. Creativity is definitely a strength of this organization. The challenge was to persuade everyone that their creativity was not only welcome but expected, a goal I knew that Tom and Kate were committed to.

With my research results in hand, I began creating a "grid" listing six skills that I believed would be valuable to see at Tom's of Maine, along with how that skill might fit in at Tom's. I also included the general "orientation" of each skill. The skill of leadership in this organization, for example, would require "humility and the willingness to venture out." Creativity needs "flexibility and persistence." My goal was to give employees a list of skills to refer to that would help them talk to each other about what they were good at. In the process, it became clear how centered the company had become around our statements of the mission, beliefs, and reason for being. And since we had all been going through various stages of the Seven Intentions, my grid of skills was clearly related to those seven steps to values-centered leadership (see the Skills Grid, pp. 174–175).

Six weeks after the Consumer and Brand Development Group of ten people began this reflection and goal-setting process, I asked everyone to rate their experience on a scale of one to five (five being the highest). The process got mostly fours and fives. People were not only pleased about the outcome, they were courageous about the goals they wanted to take on and honest about the skills they needed to develop. The company's Finance and Trade Marketing Groups are now going to take a crack at the new assessment process using our materials.

Skills Grid

Orientation	Skill Category	How This Skill Might Show Up at Tom's
Humility and the Willingness to Venture Out	Servant Leadership— Leading through actions which serve the beliefs, mission, and reason for being and the community at Tom's of Maine as it seeks to fulfill its mission.	• Initiating and championing a new idea that helps us more fully realize our mission. • Taking on a task in a team that helps to serve the mission-centered purpose of the team. • Identifying and taking initiative on an idea that builds our internal community or capacity.
Flexibility and Persistence	Creativity—Releasing individual creativity and fostering it in others to create innovative products, ideas, and solutions to problems.	• Setting aside individual time for thinking through creative solutions to a problem. • Convening a group to brainstorm new ideas on a project. • Coming up with creative alternatives in the face of a series of difficult obstacles.
Openness to and with Others	Communication—Engaging in full and honest dialogue with our consumers, customers, partners, and one another.	• Engaging in an open, positive, and truthful assessment process with someone. • Sharing honest information with a consumer about our products. • Sharing honestly with a co-worker about an issue that has arisen in working with him/her. • Getting consumer comments on an idea.

Respectfulness	Interdependence— Working collaboratively with others in a way that is accountable to our beliefs, mission, and reason for being and that honors the diversity and contribution of others.	• Working productively in a team. • Providing for facilitation in a team that allows all members to contribute. • Routinely consulting others on projects that need cross-functional expertise and participation.
Passion for Action	Planning and Organization—Creating a disciplined way to get things done.	• Laying out the goals of a project and the steps needed to reach these goals. • Spending time working through a team charter. • Working with a team or group to identify specific next steps and then following up.
Curiosity and an Openness to Insight	Analysis and Identifying Opportunities— Uncovering and analyzing data that leads to insights and actions.	• Probing into data to understand how our business is doing as a starting point for planning for the future. • Reviewing information and identifying a new opportunity for Tom's of Maine. • Uncovering the facts of a particular situation or problem before outlining a potential solution.

INTENTION #6 TALKING POINTS

Every business leader is accountable, and values-centered leaders are open to an even broader assessment.

Managing Upside Down is a trial-and-error process and must be edited and constructively criticized every step of the way.

Managing Upside Down is a team process, and every member of the team should be able to criticize.

The standards of accountability are always the company's deepest values—the mission, beliefs, and reason for being statements.

Upside Down Managers have three obligations: (1) serving customers; (2) performing that service in a way that doesn't harm people, the community, or the environment; and (3) making money.

Make sure job descriptions and goals are clear—and in line with the company's values and destiny.

Review the Skills Grid (see pp. 174–175).

INTENTION #6 HOMEWORK

Think of a recent time when you took a creative risk at work. What was the most difficult thing about this? The creative part or the risk?

Now think about the boundaries, real or imagined, that you have set for yourself. These questions might help:

- How do you usually hem yourself in?
- Are there certain things you want to keep? Certain people?

- Do you have certain beliefs you never question?
- What would be the risk of moving outside your boundaries? What is your worst fear?

Decide on a creative risk you will take in your work in the near future. Then share this decision and your strategy for accomplishing it with a colleague or family member.

After you have taken this creative risk, assess it by asking the following questions:

- What was my goal?
- Was the risk based on my vision?
- Which of my key values did I express?
- Which of my key values did I set aside or ignore?
- What worked? What didn't work?
- How might I approach such a task next time? Do it differently?

Discuss the answers to these questions with the other person.

Write in your journal any affirmations that you receive from others during the workday, at home, in the community, and in any other groups you belong to.

Reflect on how your beliefs and values (current as well as those you're inclined to set aside) and the creative risk modify your vision. Then edit your vision statement accordingly.

9

Pass It On

INTENTION #7
It is our responsibility to fellow humans to be in a state of constant donation. When we receive gifts, knowledge, goodness, extra time, and profits, we are obliged to pass them along to others. In the process, we set up an exchange of experiences and a trial-and-error process that can help us all improve.

The very first package of our natural toothpaste included a message on the label—addressed to ''Dear new customers and old friends''— that told the story of the origin of Tom's of Maine, about how when Kate and I couldn't find products for our family without additives, dyes, and preservatives, we set out to create our own. Each Tom's of Maine container or carton listed the product's ingredients, in big letters. It was not the way they did it at Colgate-Palmolive or Procter & Gamble, but we knew our customers were different. Their prime concern, just like the Chappells', was what was in their products. Our first distributor, Paul Hawken, who was also our mentor, had advised us to keep our packaging simple and informational. Keeping the customer informed was a key. Pass it on!

From the beginning, we were passing on to our customers what we cared about and what we were learning. Of course, back then I hadn't developed any theory about the social and financial advantages of being so open. It was just the way we were. I guess we Chappells have always been an opinionated, talky bunch. Eventually our packaging was covered with messages, discussing our definition of ''natural,'' explaining the active natural ingredients in the product (calcium carbonate in toothpaste, for example), their purpose (mild abrasive), and their source (purified calcium from the earth). It was only years later, when we moved onto supermarket and drugstore shelves, that marketing research confirmed our intuitions. Focus groups revealed that our customers liked knowing what the ingredients were, where they came from, and what their purpose was. They loved hearing about why Kate and I went into the natural personal care products business.

When the company started doing radio commercials, we discovered that the more personal they were, the better our audience liked them. (One actually featured my own mother reporting that when I was a child I gave her a hard time about brushing my teeth because the toothpaste was too sweet.) It wasn't long before the company was including with its packaging informational inserts and outserts keeping people up to date on our volunteer work and charitable donations along with relaying stories from customers who had written to us about their experiences with Tom's of Maine products. There followed *Common Good Reports*, a kind of Upside Down annual report on the company's philanthropy and environmental projects. And now, of course, we have our own website, www.tomsof maine.com. (We're getting three thousand hits a month.)

By passing it on, we created a community of Tom's of Maine customers that was a lot more diverse than Kate and I could ever have imagined in the early days. We have kept expanding that community. More important, our customers began telling us that one of the reasons they bought our products was because they liked our company's commitment to people and the environment. In short, they liked our values. That was an important moment for me. Suddenly I realized that I had something to tell my colleagues in the business world. For years, so-called experts had been warning me that I was doing things the wrong way. Why didn't I list the benefits of my products on the packages? Who would want to buy an unsweetened natural toothpaste? You're nuts to take on the big toothpaste companies! We did, we succeeded, and I realized that the big boys might be able to learn a thing or two from Tom's of Maine.

I began giving more speeches. More and more business leaders were asking me if I could spare some time to discuss my ideas with them. I decided to write a book about why and how I began to let our values drive the company. Since then, I've learned a lot more about managing by values, some of it the hard way. Frankly, I thought it would be a lot easier. But I've been making it up as I've gone along, learning by trial and error, seeking advice from wiser souls. One of the toughest, most personally frustrating lessons I've learned is that a few professional managers are born values-centered, a few more may be raised with the right values, but most have to learn how to do it. If I wanted my people to be as values-centered as I am, then I would have to train them. To that end, I have devised these Seven Intentions.

But because I think Tom's of Maine is on to something important, I want to put my tools out there for everyone to use, to edit, and to try to create a different kind of way of doing business, *a new paradigm* of interconnected partnerships. Internally, the organization is no longer a hierarchy with power concentrated at the top of the corporate pyramid, forcing the departments to struggle constantly for position and favor. The company is now a system of fluid, interlocking relationships built around trust and accountability. At the center, holding the system together, are the company's values.

To spread the word about this new paradigm for corporate culture, I have set up a nonprofit educational foundation, The Saltwater Institute, which will eventually offer workshops all around the country to business people interested in learning how to Manage Upside Down.

All learning is progressive. We learn from those who have gone before; even geniuses, as the old saying goes, stand on other people's shoulders. I believe that it's a human responsibility to share knowledge. CEOs have traditionally been very protective about their ideas and breakthroughs. When the game is all about winning (i.e., making the most money possible), why give the competition your edge? Managing by values, however, is not all about winning or increasing the bottom line. There's no need to hold back your formula for success. In fact, because values-centered managers care about people before money, we are morally bound to share our ideas. For me, Managing Upside Down is a constant process of donation, exchanging experiences, learning from trial and error, and then passing on your results.

WE'RE NOT "MASTERS OF THE UNIVERSE," WE'RE ITS SERVANTS

The writer Tom Wolfe dubbed them "masters of the universe," the sharp players on Wall Street during the greedy 1980s whom Wolfe skewered in his bestselling novel of bad manners, *The Bonfire of the Vanities*. We Upside Down Managers are not in the business of lording over anyone, let alone the universe. At Tom's of Maine, we have set a strategic imperative to respect people and nature. It is our job to serve our customers and the community. The company's mission is centered on this concept of servanthood.

As I began marshaling my thoughts about Intention #7, we held a meeting of the entire company, all eighty-five of us assembled in one big room. It was an effort to discuss the "reason for being" we had drafted for Tom's of Maine, along with our future vision and our strategic plan to get us there. This was not one of those meetings where the officers of the company stand up to make presentations to everyone else seated in rows of chairs. The plan was to make this daylong session highly interactive, with lots of circles and workshops that would encourage community and intimacy. We were eager to find out what employees were learning in their assigned roles; we also wanted to get a sense of their take on where the company was going and how well they understood the strategic principles that were supposed to get us to that destination.

The people who spoke were from every area of the company. One of my administrative assistants, Gail Burgess, presented her understanding of the concept of servanthood as having enough confidence in yourself not to let your own pride get in the way of helping others, whether co-workers, family members, or neighbors. And so it went throughout the day, as people from all parts of the company stood up before a large group, some for the first time in their lives, to say, "Here is what I've done." We heard about ideas for new products, about new alliances with other organizations, including nonprofits, to do things related to our common values. For the first time, the employees heard about the idea of a campus for Tom's of Maine, a new company headquarters that would be a community dedicated to natural living, education, and creativity, as well as a successful and profitable business enterprise.

Tom O'Brien and I had worked for months preparing for this meeting, hiring outside facilitators to help us design the program and run it. It was a kind of "Pass It On" festival. My part was to report about how the owners and the board came to recommit to the private ownership of the company. I shared the story about the Chappell family meetings where we discussed the prospect of moving into such new businesses as natural skin care, personal wellness, and even pet care. I explained how pharmacognosy could help put us in those businesses. I told everyone how we had a clear vision of what was possible. It was the first time I had spoken publicly about this new picture of Tom's of Maine, and I asked everyone to commit themselves to the "Six Imperatives" required for us to achieve our new goals.

While I had my say (and so did Tom O'Brien), the meeting turned out to be very much a kind of metaphor for the obligation to pass it on. It was a powerful day, the most significant meeting we've ever had as a company. Immersed in the values of the company and the stories others told about living those values, you had to emerge from the meeting as more connected to those values and, as a result, more fully rounded by them. You might be a Tom's of Maine engineer, but you didn't come out of this experience as just an engineer. You had become both an engineer and a wiser human being.

That's what happens when you pass it on.

THE TWO PRINCIPLES OF PASSING IT ON

The first is *the idea of uncertainty*. Managing Upside Down, as I noted in the previous chapter, is a new ball game. We are learning by trial and error. That is why assessment is so important. We want to make sure we're not heading down the wrong road. That's the self-interested part. The socially responsible part is that we also want to share our burdens as well as our successes to help others not only to learn but also to build on the model. If managing by values is managing in uncertainty, then no one has all the answers. We're all finding our way. You cannot learn this style of management in a business school. It's a new and different way, which is why I like calling it Managing Upside Down. It turns all the rules on their heads, starting with the first principle of classic capitalism: Profit is king.

In Managing Upside Down, knowledge is not power, wisdom is. Knowledge is the product of education, whereas wisdom comes from the experience of operating with shared values. The values-centered company moves forward step by step, coping with uncertainty, learning as it goes along, trying and erring, creating the guidebook on the way. Traditional corporations are often too quick to jettison their most experienced managers in favor of the young whiz kids brandishing all the latest tools from business school. For the graybeards around the office, it's up and out. What a waste of wisdom!

Tom O'Brien is twenty years younger than I am. He has a Harvard MBA and top-level leadership and marketing experience in a huge international company. But we spend at least six hours a week alone discussing the business. He raises new ideas for our strategy and reports on how current plans are being executed. I am learning a lot from him, but he also wants to hear from me. He says he enjoys spending time with me and Kate as well as our long-time plant manager and head of production, Gary Rittershaus. Our experience, he says, gives perspective to his decision-making. In a values-centered company we're exploring new territory. And when you head into the deepest jungle without a map, you need experienced and wise guides.

And thus the second principle of passing it on: *Teach what you have learned.* Teaching others is not an entirely altruistic step, because by teaching you are not only conveying your wisdom to someone else, you are learning more about your ideas. What better way to understand what you are doing than to have to explain it to someone else? When I convey my success to others, it actually makes me more conscious of what is working on my end. When I explain my failures, I am bound to get a sharper grasp on where I went wrong. By teaching, I also provide a context for future dialogue. My audience begins to understand where I'm coming from; at the very least, we are now talking the same language. Better still, my listeners may recognize similarities in what they're doing, or point out that their experience is quite different.

Passing it on is a two-way street. We become teachers and students. I like to think of this as an exchange of experiences where we each evolve to a higher understanding. And we're wiser for the exchange. Managing Upside Down is not a competition. We're all in it together. All of us wisdom-seekers realize how quickly we can forget what we know in the daily struggle in the marketplace. Who is not susceptible to human frailty, greed, the abuse of power, and what Shakespeare's Hamlet called "the insolence of office"? When people come to Kate and me for advice, we know that their very presence and conversation will keep us on track with our values. And if they think our thinking or decisions have strayed, they need not fear speaking up. All they have to do is point to the mission.

No secrets here. Tom's of Maine is so intent on letting the sun shine in that we have stipulated that part of our reason for being is "to help create a better world by exchanging with others our faith, experience, and hope." Faith—what place does that have in business? I'm not talking about religion, but a commitment to what we're doing *even though we are not certain we have it absolutely right.* As I keep saying, Managing Upside Down is not physics. You cannot learn it in business school. Even a book like this can only be a guide. You have to learn it by doing it. Managing Upside Down is what I like to call a "home art," something that you can learn on your own and get better at through practice. And so we have to have a certain measure of faith in what we're doing. Our wisdom comes from our on-the-job experience. Hope is what gets us out of bed in the morning.

THE FULL CIRCLE OF THE SEVEN INTENTIONS
Being secretive and selfish goes against the very nature of a values-centered company. A company driven by its values is a morally responsible (and responsive) company. Morality, by definition, is a social practice. And while traditional companies believe they are in business for the money, a company driven by values knows that social and environmental responsibilities must come first.

Tom's of Maine has built on its mission and beliefs statements to where we have articulated a reason for being whose first principle stresses our social role "to serve our customers' health needs with imaginative science from plants and minerals." That requires us to put aside our pride (Intention #1), get to know ourselves (Intention #2) and turn that expertise into the focus of our business. Why bother to try to sell products unrelated to your specialty? You must step up and accept your destiny (Intention #3), get the advice that helps you do it right (Intention #4), and then go for it, venturing out into the marketplace to take your chances (Intention #5) and measuring yourself against the gold standard of your values (Intention #6). That ties into our second reason for being, which is "to inspire all those we serve with a mission of responsibility and goodness.'' This requires letting our suppliers and customers know what our mission is so that we can build partnerships within the retail trade.

One of the simplest and fastest ways to build such a partnership is to identify values that you and your retail partners share. Central to our system of beliefs and values at Tom's of Maine is a commitment to communities. We have set out to collaborate with retail customers who are equally as committed to the common good as Tom's of Maine, in an effort to remind our customers that we're both trying to get involved in the life of our own communities. In 1997, Tom's of Maine gave a modest grant to the Jane Goodall Institute. We then followed up by featuring in our inserts JGI's Roots & Shoots environmental and humanitarian program, teaching young people from preschool to college age all over the world ''to make the world a better place for animals, the environment, and the human community.'' In a 1998 insert, we included a coupon and told our customers that if they returned it, we would donate a dollar on their behalf to JGI. We received over one thousand coupons. In the next year's insert, we encouraged Tom's of Maine consumers to start Roots & Shoots programs in their own schools and communities. In return, we promised to pay the $25 startup fee. This collaboration between Tom's of Maine and the Jane Goodall Institute has helped to bring Roots and Shoots programs to many communities around the country.

Later that year, my daughter Sarah, who had been a fan of Jane Goodall's work long before she joined the company and had worked closely with JGI on the Roots and Shoots promotion, learned that KTCA, the PBS station in Minneapolis, was planning a one-hour television program on Jane Goodall pegged to the September 1999 publication of a book she had written about her life. We decided to get involved as a corporate underwriter of this TV documentary about Jane Goodall's lifelong commitment to nature entitled *Reason for Hope*. By the spring of 1999, we had agreed to be the sole underwriter, donating $400,000 to KTCA for the film's production costs; we also decided to ante up another $400,000 in promotional costs. We are planning a big campaign to alert the public about *Reason for Hope* through our outsert/insert program and Common Good Partnerships with our retail customers. We have also created posters and promotions for the PBS program.

What's in it for us? Well, spending money on such a project cannot be justified in any kind of measurable return on investment. Tom's of Maine is not a commercial advertiser that has bought a certain number of TV spots to promote our products. But in qualitative terms, bankrolling a film that will celebrate the life and values of Jane Goodall, a woman who has devoted her life to promoting respect for all living things, is a bull's-eye for a company like Tom's of Maine. We share with Jane Goodall the mission to raise public consciousness about respecting each other and the environment; our company is committed to the notion that businesses must become stewards of the kind of humanitarian and environmental responsibility that Jane Goodall embodies. What better way to "inspire all those we serve with a mission of responsibility and goodness" than to partner up with the Jane Goodall Institute? Sarah advised that it was a perfect fit, and Tom O'Brien and I championed the idea and found a way to pay for it. Over the next year, *Reason for Hope* will be the centerpiece of our mission.

The Goodall partnership also feeds right into the third element in our reason for being: "to empower others by sharing our knowledge, time, talents, and profits." Donating our time and money is now a longstanding habit at Tom's of Maine. When we began, we could have never imagined giving away almost a million dollars, but today underwriting and promoting *Reason for Hope* seems like such a natural step for our company. Pass it on! Which brings us back to Intention #7.

The Seven Intentions create another circle. We begin by setting aside our pride and self-interest by connecting to a force bigger than we are, goodness (Intention #1), which encourages us to find our values by getting to know ourselves (Intention #2). Self-knowledge helps us determine what our gifts are and thus what kind of company we should be (Intention #3). We confirm that by seeking advice (Intention #4), and then we venture out into the marketplace to take our chances (Intention #5), all the while checking on ourselves, assessing what we're doing against our only gold standard, our values (Intention #6). "How'm I doing?," as a New York City mayor once famously used to walk the city's streets and ask. If you're doing well and if you're learning more about how to get your values to drive your business, then you have an obligation to let others know how to do it (Intention #7). Pass it on!

The Seven Intentions themselves are connected. They flow from each other and then circle back, stressing that the Seven Intentions is a neverending process. You do not graduate from the Seven Intentions.

But you do keep passing it on. This final step underlines the most fundamental constant of our new kind of capitalism—that doing business is a *social and interconnected* enterprise. And if we think our own businesses ought to be responsible to our communities and to society, then we can encourage other businesses accordingly. Not all will agree. (Remember the remark from Al Dunlap I quoted in Chapter 1 that "business is not a social experiment.") I believe it's our job as values-centered leaders to try to persuade those in our path that business can be a socially conscious enterprise as well as a profitable one.

Which, of course, sends us right back to Intention #1. For what better way to forego your pride and connect to goodness than to pass it on and serve others?

PASSING IT ON PAYS YOU BACK

My principle is: "If you don't pass it along, you lose it." How so? When you keep to yourself something that could benefit others or society as a whole, you have bought into the bottom-line thinking that promotes isolation and dominance, all the things that values-centered leaders hope to put behind them. Passing it on reinforces each of us to carry our faith into the next day. Telling others about what you're doing might open you up to something you didn't know or alert you to a problem that is lurking down the road. There's also the possibility that your biggest problem might have already been solved by someone else. And when we pass our experience along, we become recipients, unexpectedly, of more gifts from the universe.

Here we can learn much from the worlds of research and scholarship. Historically, the reason why scholars publish their findings is to alert the rest of the community to their breakthroughs and thus expand the boundaries of their field. Scientists, in particular, are dependent on the work of their colleagues to push the envelope of scientific knowledge further. We are now partners with the American Health Foundation, one of the nation's leading research facilities for the prevention of diseases. Their researchers are constantly building on each other's work. They pass along their results to outside partners and affiliates. And while scientists are no less eager than business people to get there first, the last thing any researcher wants to do is to spend months, maybe even years, reinventing the wheel. The solution is to talk about your work and publish.

It is called "the pursuit of knowledge," and it cannot be done in secret. Pass it on!

Intention #6 was about assessing things honestly. And publicly. While secrecy and discretion may have a place in assessing individual performance, the furtive values-centered company is a contradiction in terms. Why assess something and not tell people your results? The very idea of a secret organizational assessment suggests distortion, ulterior motives, and a dangerous lack of accountability. But when assessment is appropriately public, it promotes responsibility and harnesses the thoughtful insights and critiques that come from a variety of perspectives. At Tom's of Maine we believe that even individuals can benefit and grow from evaluations that, while not being totally public, are passed on to the individual and his key relationships in the company.

LEARNING HOW TO PASS IT ON

Passing it on is simply a more public (and sometimes published) version of the urge everyone has to tell his or her story. Storytelling is a very important part of our lives at Tom's of Maine. Every company is a community, and we will never know anything about our colleagues unless we listen to their stories.

When was the last time you had a real conversation with one of your co-workers, not about the weather or about your favorite sports team, but about your lives? Hierarchy cuts against community; job titles can make people, even those with similar interests, uncomfortable. The bigger the company, the more rigid these categories. Corporations give a lot of lip service to being a "family," but it's usually the kind of family where daddy (the CEO) has the final word. To the contrary, the values-centered organization realizes that if you do try to treat one another as you would a real family member, listen to their stories about their lives, their joys, and their tragedies, you will engender relationships that enrich not only you but also your company. In any happy family, people must talk to each other. I see sharing what's going on in one's life and work as the mark of a happy, expressive, and complete soul.

The wonderful thing about learning is that unless you've passed it on, you haven't truly learned it. An idea does not really gain its potency in your mind and experience until you have thought it through, understood it, and reshaped it in a way that you can pass on to someone else.

To help you understand this, I recommend a learning exercise that you can do in a small group or even with another person. Pick a personal topic such as, "What do I value about myself?" "What are my skills?" "What are my gifts?" "What do I need to work on?" You then give your answer, which your partner listens to and then plays back to you. The revelation comes in hearing someone else repeat your own take on yourself. Most of us (maybe all of us) do not fully own the things we say about ourselves until we share them with others. When these traits get repeated, when we actually experience them in public, they begin to take hold as things we really value about ourselves.

This kind of experiential learning is more productive when we have to reenact what others have said about us. Of course, most people tend to be a little shy talking about themselves in public. You have to get the ball rolling, and I've found that one effective way to inspire people to reveal themselves and what they value is to ask them who their heroes and heroines are and explain why. In that company meeting I mentioned earlier, we broke up into pairs during a discussion of Tom's of Maine's reason for being to talk among ourselves about our own reasons for being. What was it about us as individuals that we thought was important, unique? I was paired with a woman who told me that though she valued being a wife and mother, she didn't think that completed the essence of who she was. At the age of forty, she was searching for that certain something that would satisfy this craving to be more than a wife and mother.

One of her heroines, she said, was Maria Montessori, the Italian educator whose experiential and interactive learning methods for young children have spread around the world. My partner spoke of her own deep commitment to the idea that there are different ways to learn than those that are emphasized in our public school system. My partner felt so deeply about justice for all people that she admitted that sometimes she could see herself as a radical like Malcolm X, the black leader who was murdered in 1965 after he broke from the Nation of Islam to begin organizing a more broadly based political program aimed at social justice for African-Americans. At other times, she found herself drawn to Mother Teresa, the Catholic nun who had devoted herself to the poorest of the poor of India.

What better way to think through your gifts and goals in life than explaining them to a friend? Once you hear yourself saying these things and then your partner repeating them in public, you begin to think seriously about taking the next step to make your dreams a reality. Seeing how inspiring the Seven Intentions were and how they were changing lives in Boulder and Kennebunk, I began to think of other ways of passing on what we have been learning at Tom's of Maine about Managing Upside Down. After all, I believe so strongly in managing by values that I've put our company on the line. To train our managers to live their company's values, I devised the Seven Intentions. To spread the word, I continued to speak to audiences all around the country and began thinking about getting the Seven Intentions down in book form. But I soon realized that I myself had a limited amount of time for proselytizing. (I still had a business to run.) I began to explore another way of passing on the Seven Intentions.

INSTITUTIONALIZING INTENTION #7

In 1996, when I started working with the Boulder Business Group, it occurred to me that Tom's of Maine could create an actual training center where business people could immerse themselves in the Seven Intentions. One of the reasons I got involved with the Boulder Business Group was that I knew that thinking about how to integrate values into the marketplace is difficult to do on your own. It was better to be in dialogue with a group of like-minded people. If you think of the traditional way of doing business, the single-minded pursuit of profit, as a kind of bad habit (and for some a terrible addiction), then trying to break that bad habit will require support. Mentioning to colleagues that you'd like to integrate your personal values into your work can sometimes provoke derision. It might even be risky for your career. Maybe you have tried to be more values-centered but feel that your actions are not consistent with what you believe in. We all need help in breaking down the forces around us that are constantly whispering the refrain, "Maximize profit, maximize profit." Frankly, the experience is a lot like the concept of a support group for any obsession.

Knowing from personal experience how crucial the support and encouragement of other people who are trying to break the same bad habits can be, I decided to create a support group for people who wanted to manage in a more values-centered way. I would give them a tool kit that would help reorient their business habits, the Seven Intentions. But I would also give them the fellowship of other Upside Down managers to encourage them on their new journey. I decided to call it The Saltwater Institute. (Living near the coast of Maine and being an avid sailor, I've always loved the distinctive fragrance of saltwater. For me, saltwater has always felt cleansing, making you feel fresh, and that was exactly the effect I wanted this Saltwater Institute to have on my fellow business managers eager to try a new way of doing business.)

I went to my board for advice. They were intrigued and began to see The Saltwater Institute as a potential profit center. Tom's of Maine had learned so much about managing by values, why not sell what we learned? Their enthusiasm certainly confirmed my feeling that I had a good idea. But I resisted going commercial. I know that training in the Seven Intentions has the power to transform people and institutions, and I didn't want people to think our aim was to turn them into a clone of Tom's of Maine. And I certainly didn't want them to think that the Seven Intentions was just another Tom's of Maine product.

My instinct was to make The Saltwater Institute a not-for-profit organization. Yes, I considered the fact that we were a commercial company and that private enterprise was what we understood. But as a businessman who has worked closely with many nonprofits and shares values with them, I also learned that while you can expand people's awareness of your toothpaste only in direct proportion to the amount of money you spend on advertising, goodness travels like wildfire. It knows no limits. I also realized that the fastest grow-ing spiritual movement in America was twelve-step therapy. It's not a company selling a product or a club inviting you to join. Entering twelve-step therapy is up to the individual. The price of entry is also up to you. If you want help with a particular obsession or addiction, then you go to that meeting to work with those people who have the same affliction as you do. It is a highly effective system. It is in every market. It is not for profit.

That was how I began to see the Seven Intentions. I wanted this kind of training to be available everywhere and to everyone, including my competitors. If training in the Seven Intentions was as effective as I believed it could be, I wanted it available to global companies as well as to small entrepreneurs. The Saltwater Institute should not be cloaked in a Tom's of Maine garment. It had to have its own identity and its own board of directors. I sought the advice of John Whitehead, who had recently retired as the chairman of the New York investment banking firm of Goldman Sachs. I had gotten to know John through our work with the Episcopal church. He has the special wisdom of a man who has managed to live the life of a great capitalist *and* a great Christian. John Whitehead has become a friend and a mentor, and I am inclined to listen to him. To ensure objectivity, accessibility, and an open invitation to everyone, no matter what company they worked for, John advised that we set up a 501c-3 educational foundation separate from Tom's of Maine. "Otherwise," he said, "Tom's of Maine would be a barrier to your success." He also pointed out that as an educational foundation The Saltwater Institute would be able to attract foundation grants as well as grants from private companies who wanted to help.

I decided to go the nonprofit way. That meant a new and diverse board of directors not governed by Tom's of Maine. It also meant building alliances with people who had gone through the Seven Intentions pilot projects in Boulder and Kennebunk who were as enthusiastic as I to see a center for Seven Intentions training come to life. We incorporated The Saltwater Institute in the fall of 1998 with a board of four men and three women who are either currently running a business or had done so in the past. Each has had an interesting journey related to values and/or the education of values. (Only three of the group are from Tom's of Maine, two members of the board plus myself.) I put together a "Co-Founder's Circle" of fifteen graduates of the Seven Intentions, who immediately went to work drafting beliefs and mission statements (see boxes on pp. 211 and 212). We envisioned various kinds of services such a foundation might offer in addition to the Seven Intentions training, and we developed a business plan.

Saltwater is now fully operational, with headquarters in Boulder and Boston and its own website, www.saltwater.org. We intend to add four or five more cities that will be serviced by West and East Coast teams of facilitators. As we kick off the first programs, we will be simultaneously teaching additional Seven Intentions trainers to operate in the new cities. My plan is to eventually have Saltwater Institute centers in thirty or so cities. Saltwater is not designed to be a five-day executive retreat. The kind of change we are fostering can occur only gradually, learning with the same group of people at the same time. Each group will take on one intention during a single four-hour session every three weeks. Everyone requires plenty of time to process what they're learning, and we believe in homework. Each person is assigned a buddy to work with between meetings. To fulfill the institute's mission "to create an ongoing fellowship of Seven Intentions practitioners," Saltwater will allow graduates to return regularly for recharging by spending time with new trainees. We also plan to hold regular discussions on the usual dilemmas that come up in business around our central issue: "How do you learn to Manage Upside Down?" Special workshops on related topics such as creativity will be offered.

The Saltwater Institute will be a learning center, a support circle, and a fellowship, not a would-be graduate school. For trainees inspired by their Seven Intentions training to probe deeper into the academic literature on values and ethics, we hope to set up alliances with related university programs such as the Harvard Divinity School's Center for the Study of Values in Public Life.

TOWARD A NEW PARADIGM

In my travels around the country speaking about values-centered leadership, I have seen it and felt it. I have heard it point-blank from business people I have talked to. People are frustrated with the system. They find the traditional hierarchical corporation too limited, too competitive, and too one-dimensional. How do we change that? Can we evolve from a hierarchy in which the power and the knowledge are perceived to reside at the top to a system built around core values and a new mission? I believe we can—but only if we pioneers, undaunted by the trial-and-error process and open to the many and diverse perspectives provided by partnerships and teamwork, lead the way.

We need new ideas all around. My contribution is in the area of changing American business, to broaden its orientation from a single-minded focus on the bottom line to a more inclusive approach that builds value with values by integrating social and environmental responsibilities with the pursuit of profit. If you've read this far, you are likely to have a sense of how powerful the Seven Intentions can be. This is a system that can change people and organizations. Of course, these days everyone makes that pitch: This new car will make you a new person, that hairdo will do it, that plastic surgeon, this cereal, not to mention the stuff in this little bottle. But the ideas in this book are more than a wild bit of self-promotion on my part. I know how revolutionary the ideas in this program are because I have watched them transform my own company (and me).

This transformative power makes the Seven Intentions more than a gimmick for making a company more values-centered, more profitable, or even simply a more interesting place to spend your days earning a living. It is much more than a new twist on business as usual, like dress-down Fridays, say, or allowing some employees to telecommute. Managing the values-centered way goes a lot deeper into the essence of what the corporation ought to be. Creating values-driven companies is a whole new way of looking at a brand of capitalism that has been in history's driver's seat since the middle of the nineteenth century.

In 1889, the steel tycoon Andrew Carnegie promoted a socio-economic theory that managed to combine the traditional doctrine of Christian stewardship with arguments against any public interference in the typically American values of individualism, competition, and the accumulation of wealth and private property. Observers at the time noted that the great Carnegie had articulated a "gospel of wealth" that was both true and very American. Free-market capitalism, they argued, was not only the American way, it was also the Christian way. And while a few dissenters among Protestant religious leaders called for a more "social Christianity," most of their colleagues, Catholic and Jewish as well as Protestant, supported Carnegie's view that the primary aim of government was to nurture and increase economic growth. Businessmen of the day (and in those days, of course, business was a men's only club) believed that the benefits of their prosperity would trickle down to the community. A century later, it's a version of capitalism that still reigns supreme.

My aim is to turn that view of capitalism upside down. I am delighted to cast my lot with the dissenters of Carnegie's day. And I can't tell you how much I enjoy the fact (and the irony) that in 1989, one hundred years after Carnegie was promoting his gospel of wealth, I convinced the capitalists on my board of directors that Tom's of Maine had a mission "to be a profitable and successful company, while acting in a socially and environmentally responsible manner." We decided that business could also be in the business of working for the common good as well as for profit. That means caring about other people as people. We decided that our company would aspire to be not a "master of the universe" but its servant. Sure, we can't survive without capital. But I would expand capital to include human capital (as some economists already do), social capital, and moral capital—namely, the human, social, and moral (and religious and spiritual) resources that bond every society on earth and make us productive no less than financial capital does.

I believe that those of us who have seen the economic and social benefits of permitting values to drive our financial strategies have to speak out on behalf of a more socially minded and compassionate kind of capitalism. On the verge of the twenty-first century, what CEO would aspire to be a nineteenth-century robber baron? (And the tycoon wannabes of today might consider the irony that these days most people know the Carnegie name best for its role in American philanthropy, not least for endowing public libraries all over America.)

As a new century begins, we have to start thinking about the next way of doing business, particularly for children like our own who have grown up respecting the environment and amid the kind of ethnic, religious, and sexual diversity that was inconceivable to my parents when I was a kid. I think Managing Upside Down is a good place to start. It is my hope that the Seven Intentions, constantly improved by experience and assessment, will provide individuals, teams, and complete companies with the tools for making themselves more inner-directed and driven not only by their pursuit of profit, but also by their values.

The Seven Intentions gives business people frustrated by the profit-only method of business a tool kit for integrating their values. Equally important, the Seven Intentions offers an answer to the question, ''Where do we go after hierarchy?'' If the idea of the omnipotent and omniscient CEO is to be junked, if the corporate pyramid is no longer an appropriate metaphor for twenty-first-century managers who know that no one man has all the answers and that companies have to be socially and morally as well as fiscally responsible, what do we replace the pyramid with?

The Seven Intentions provides the answer: *partnership.*

HOW DO YOU MOVE AWAY FROM HIERARCHY TO PARTNERSHIP?

By not having to do anything alone. That's how. It's the fundamental principle of this new paradigm of values-centered management. In the traditional hierarchical system of corporate governance that we used to have, every decision flowed through the CEO's office, like sand in an hourglass. The CEO signed off on everything. Today, we have broken the hourglass to let creativity flow through the company. The old method put all its money on the company's decision-makers. This new paradigm steps away from the ego-driven model in favor of partnerships. I believe the solution lies not in one all-powerful executive, the boss of bosses, but in two or more people in partnership with each other and the company's mission.

A Tom's of Maine partnership could be as limited as CEO Tom Chappell and COO Tom O'Brien, who are the executive leadership of the company, or as broad as our partnership teams in the areas of finance, brands, supplies, and every other group that constitutes the new organizational system of our company, which now looks like the graphic on the next page.

The engine that powers this system is the mission. Notice how the values and beliefs of the company spread weblike into every area of the corporation (notice the circles), thus breaking up the mission into specific functions, from Finance and Supply down to the R&D acorns. The graphic illustrates our key principles of interconnectedness, interdependency, inner-driven generativity, and trust and accountability. No area of the company operates without an eye on the mission and belief statements. Any employee on any team can drive the process, generate new ideas, and suggest new products because the company's values, beliefs, and goals—its destiny—are no secret. Every circle in the system, every team, has the same target in its sights.

But the key that ignites this engine of partnership is the dual principle of trust and accountability. I cannot pass any responsibility to Tom O'Brien unless I trust that he will act according to the company's core values and work toward the destiny of our mission. Similarly, as leaders, Tom and I cannot let go of any of our responsibility unless we trust the beliefs and the mission of the people we're counting on. And so it goes, as you let responsibility flow out through

Tom's of Maine
Organizational System

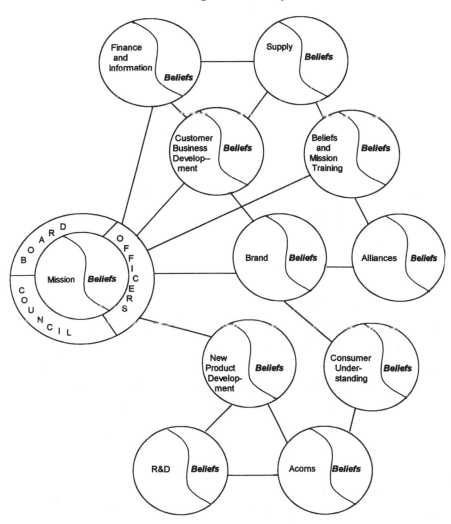

Partners in Mission
- **interdependent**
- **inner-driven generativity**

PARTNERS

this web of interrelationships, empowering others whom you trust will guard the core values of the enterprise.

It is a simple way to think. Not so long ago, I was involved in every single decision that got made at Tom's of Maine. Now, every day, meetings are going on all around me, strategies are being devised, decisions are being made, actions are being taken—without me. (And without Tom O'Brien.) The way that happens responsibly and effectively is to entrust every newly formed group of employees with some piece of the mission and expect them to solve the problems they run into creatively while being anchored in the company's core values.

It really works. Another way of looking at this new organizational system is in terms of energy flowing through the company. Traditionally, the CEO generated that energy. In this new partnership paradigm, the creative energy comes from employees in partnership with other employees or as members of teams carrying the spirit of the company's values and mission in all that they do. With the company's destiny in mind, they go about their business solving problems in the best way they can. This is how a company can move from the oppression of hierarchy to the openness of this new weblike model. How are we sure it's all really working? In addition to the mutual trust we're building among employees, our final backstop is a system of *accountability*—to the beliefs, values, mission, and destiny of the company. For while we may have flattened the hierarchy and committed ourselves to this new partnership system of running Tom's of Maine, we have tried to be very clear about what each person's job is, how it fits into the overall organization, and, most important, how the work we do serves the company's primary mission ''to be a profitable and successful company while acting in a socially and environmentally responsible manner.''

I believe that tapping into the creative power of your employees can be a company's greatest resource. But I am not about to say that you can run a company on consensus. Nor am I about to suggest that corporations can become pure democracies. All employees may have equal inherent worth, but they are not equal in economic value to the enterprise. In Chapter 4, I subscribed to St. Paul's advice in his First Epistle to the Corinthians that we each have to work with the gifts that God gave us. He compares such gifts to parts of the body that must work in union and harmony. In this passage, Paul seems to be suggesting that each part of the body is equal, that there is no difference in their respective values to the body as a whole. While I definitely believe that in the values-centered company, employees, each with his or her special talents, must be interdependent, I do not believe that all employees are equally valuable. I respect competence and the need to differentiate value among those competencies. Nor are all roles in a company created equal. In a marketing organization, you will need to value that part of the system more. Financial institutions are bound to put a priority on financial analysis. And in any competitive system, you need to value leadership. Someone has to be in charge; the buck has to stop somewhere.

I say to my COO, Tom O'Brien, that I am trusting him with the day-to-day management of developing customers and a growing consumer franchise in a manner consistent with the company's values, which includes profitability. At the same time, he is accountable to me for those aims. That's our deal, in writing. But we don't go our separate ways. We remain connected. That's what a partnership is all about. And in our partnership, Tom O. is the operative, and Tom C. is the coach. It is a partnership that is built on trust. And such trust feeds out into every corner of the company. We say to all our employees: "I entrust you with these core values and this company's mission, and you are accountable to me for the results guided by those values." And thus we develop a kind of mentor–student partnership with our employees as we pass along this trust. Every employee is in partnership with others, bound by trust and accountability, a kind of special yin–yang relationship between colleagues with decision-making authority in one member of the group.

For instance, Matt Chappell is the champion of the toothpaste acorn. Recently, his top priority has been coming up with a new toothpaste for people with sensitive teeth. Partnering with one of our formulation chemists, Pamela Scheeler, he discovered that the ingredient we needed to use to desensitize the part of the tooth that bothers some people when they brush is potassium nitrate. The bad news was that the most commonly available form of potassium nitrate is synthetically produced, and, of course, at Tom's of Maine, according to our statement of beliefs, "we believe in products that are safe, effective, and made of natural ingredients."

Matt, like others before him in the company, was stuck between maintaining our commitment to natural and coming up with a new product. The only way out was persistence and an additional dash of creativity. Pam set out to investigate another possibility, mined potassium nitrate. She learned that plenty was available, in Chile. But in Chile, potassium nitrate was used mainly in fertilizers. She and Matt found a Chilean company that would sell us mined potassium nitrate and also found a specialty chemical company in Missouri to receive the Chilean fertilizer-grade potassium nitrate and convert it to U.S.P. (for pharmocopeia) grade. Matt and Pam made it happen, and we are about to launch our new sensitive-teeth toothpaste with an all-natural potassium nitrate.

Matt and Pam's triumph resulted from a genuine partnership. As champion it was Matt's task to press for a natural solution, even though only a synthetic version of potassium nitrate seemed available. Pam, a formulation chemist with nine years of experience at Tom's of Maine, might have resented working with the boss's son, a nonscientist who has been with the company only six years. She could have also pointed to the fact that there seemed to be no natural source of potassium nitrate in the U.S. Instead, she began investigating potassium nitrate until she found a source. That it was in Chile did not deter Pam or Matt, either. They also overcame the obstacle of the potassium nitrate being fertilizer-grade by convincing the Missouri chemical company that figuring out how to upgrade the materials to U.S.P. standards might be another way to increase the chemical company's own business. In the old days, someone would have said that natural potassium nitrate did not exist in the U.S., and our sensitive-teeth toothpaste idea would have died on the vine. Matt and Pam, champion and scientist, used their mutual trust and faith, kept their eye on the company's commitment to "natural," and found a creative solution. It's what partnership in a company is all about.

Needless to say, a lot depends on who your employees are. This is a lesson we learned the hard way at Tom's of Maine, as I have revealed throughout this book. If you can hire competent people who can learn the values of the company, not just memorize them but internalize them, then you will have a winning formula. But if you hire fear-driven control freaks, they will shut the system down. If you hire ego-driven stars, they, too, will shut the system down. This new paradigm works only for those who have the humility to defer to the center of the enterprise—the company's beliefs and mission.

A NEW LEADER FOR A NEW MILLENNIUM

The obstacles that Matt and Pam ran into are familiar to everyone in business. But they broke through the barrier by sticking to the company's values. No one had to tell them how to do it. The company's values said that synthetic would not do. Any outside observer of their achievement would have to say that they did their job in a way in which we are all called on to do our work—with integrity. How can the rest of us not be equally inspired to that same kind of integrity? That's the power of example.

The Seven Intentions teaches leadership by example. In this new paradigm of business, leadership is not about hierarchy. It is not about someone at the top telling you what to do or how to execute a particular strategy. It's about putting your values together to solve today's problems. And when you see people do that, you want to know them and how they did that. You want to follow their example.

That's what I mean by the wisdom of experience. When people solve a problem, when they figure out something for the first time, the rest of us can benefit from their experience. Who doesn't want that? At Tom's of Maine, through trial and error, we have been figuring out how to do business in a new way, the values-centered way.

It can be done. Is it easy? No. Does it require a new mindset? Definitely. Will every employee you hire get it? No way. Will you have to transform the way you do business? Absolutely. Is it unconventional? You bet. But as you know, the big breakthroughs in business do not come by doing it the conventional way. You have to break the mold, create a new paradigm.

To the naysayers, I say, Don't take me at my word. Look at what we've done at Tom's of Maine. In two books, I have given a detailed and public account of how we do business. I am not keeping any secrets. How do you get your product on the shelves of thirty thousand stores? How do you take market share from some of the biggest companies in the world? How do you attract the finest talent available? How do you inspire creativity from all your employees? And how do you grow from a company with $30 million in sales to $100 million over the next three years, which is what our current plan calls for?

How do you do all that? Well, this is not just a story about a nice little company in Maine. The company that is doing all of the above is becoming an emerging force in Main Street America because we are accountable to our owners, our employees, our customers, our community, and our environment. If we can meet all those social and moral obligations and turn a sizable profit, who is to say that Managing Upside Down is not an acceptable way of conducting commerce?

THE SALTWATER STATEMENT OF BELIEFS

The co-founders of The Saltwater Institute drafted and approved this statement in September 1998.

We Believe That:

Responsible human beings and societies are structured around the following commonly held values:

- family and community responsibility,
- respect and appreciation for the natural world,
- service and stewardship,
- the necessity for work and productivity,
- an intentional commitment to goodness.

Enterprises, both for-profit and nonprofit, carry a responsibility to create and pursue missions that reflect and further the above-stated values and thus protect the common goodness and best interests of all people;

Organizational leaders can achieve, through mindfulness and intention, an integration of the shared values above with the aims of their enterprises, including high performance and profit;

Values-centered organizations and leaders are sustained by open learning environments where all people can contribute to their fullest and by actions that are consistent with their beliefs and values.

THE SALTWATER MISSION

The Saltwater Institute's Mission Is:

To research, develop, and market continuous, experience-based learning models for use in values-centered leadership and organizations;

To teach leaders the craft of integrating organizational, financial, and social good through a practicum called "The Seven Intentions of Values-Centered Leadership";

To create an ongoing fellowship of Seven Intentions practitioners and teams that provide opportunities for sharing values-centered experiences, stories, and best practices;

To evolve and improve our services through ongoing assessment, learning, and sharing of experience;

To collaborate and build alliances with all those exploring ways to shape for-profit and nonprofit enterprises to integrate financial, organizational, and social values;

To employ goodness, caring, and celebration in all our affairs as a demonstration of the added value created by the integration of social, organizational, and financial aims.

INTENTION #7 TALKING POINTS

Society can progress toward a higher standard; passing on what works helps build that progressive society.

All learning is progressive. When you have a good idea that will benefit people and the community at large, you ought to share it.

Managing Upside Down is a new way of doing business. Two main principles must guide us toward establishing this *new paradigm*:

(1) Managing by values is managing in uncertainty, and that means no one has all the answers. Knowledge is not power. The wisdom of experience is.

(2) Teach what you have learned.

To create this new paradigm, we must put the tools out there for everyone to use, to edit, and to improve in every way possible.

Managing Upside Down is built on the concept of servanthood.

The Upside Down enterprise is a real family that talks to each other and listens to people's stories about their lives.

We practitioners of values-centered leadership have to help each other. Like scientists, we have to build on others' work.

PASS IT ON!

INTENTION #7 HOMEWORK

By this stage, you've stuck with the Seven Intentions and have already felt the results of learning how to manage the values-centered way. It's now time to think about the whole process, review its effects, and contemplate the changes these principles have made in you and your work. To inspire you, here are a few questions. (For the final Intention, I'm willing to go easy on the homework.)

How has the Seven Intentions process enhanced your sense of personal empowerment to better serve your organization?

What kind of institutional changes can you suggest so that your organization can become a place where the Seven Intentions is a living, working sensibility in the culture of your organization? Be specific. And be creative.

Write down any new ideas you might have picked up on your journey to values-centered leadership that might help the rest of us. Remember: We're all operating in uncertainty, Managing Upside Down is a trial-and-error process, and we need all the help we can get. PASS IT ON!

One final thing: Congratulations! You probably picked up this book because, like me, you were looking for more meaning in your work. If you've made it this far in the Seven Intentions, you have had the opportunity to envision a whole new destiny. Step into it.

TOM'S OF MAINE MISSION

- To serve our customers by providing safe, effective, innovative, natural products of high quality.
- To build relationships with our customers that extend beyond product usage to include full and honest dialogue, responsiveness to feedback, and the exchange of information about products and issues.
- To respect, value, and serve not only our customers, but also our coworkers, owners, agents, suppliers, and our community; to be concerned about and contribute to their well-being; and to operate with integrity so as to be deserving of their trust.
- To provide meaningful work, fair compensation, and a safe, healthy work environment that encourages openness, creativity, self-discipline, and growth.
- To contribute to and affirm a high level of commitment, skill, and effectiveness in the work community.
- To recognize, encourage, and seek a diversity of gifts and perspectives in our worklife.
- To acknowledge the value of each person's contribution to our goals and to foster teamwork in our tasks.
- To be distinctive in products and policies which honor and sustain our natural world.
- To address community concerns, in Maine and around the globe, by devoting a portion of our time, talents, and resources to the environment, human needs, the arts, and education.
- To work together to contribute to the long-term value and sustainability of our company.
- To be a profitable and successful company while acting in a socially and environmentally responsible manner.

STATEMENT OF BELIEFS

- We believe that both human beings and nature have inherent worth and deserve our respect.
- We believe in products that are safe, effective, and made of natural ingredients.
- We believe that our company and our products are unique and worthwhile, and that we can sustain these genuine qualities with an ongoing commitment to innovation and creativity.
- We believe that we have a responsibility to cultivate the best relationships possible with our coworkers, customers, owners, agents, suppliers, and our community.
- We believe that different people bring different gifts and perspectives to the team and that a strong team is founded on a variety of gifts.
- We believe in providing employees with a safe and fulfilling work environment and an opportunity to grow and learn.
- We believe that competence is an essential means of sustaining our values in a competitive workplace.
- We believe our company can be financially successful while behaving in a socially responsible and environmentally sensitive manner.

Index